WELCOME
Art Class

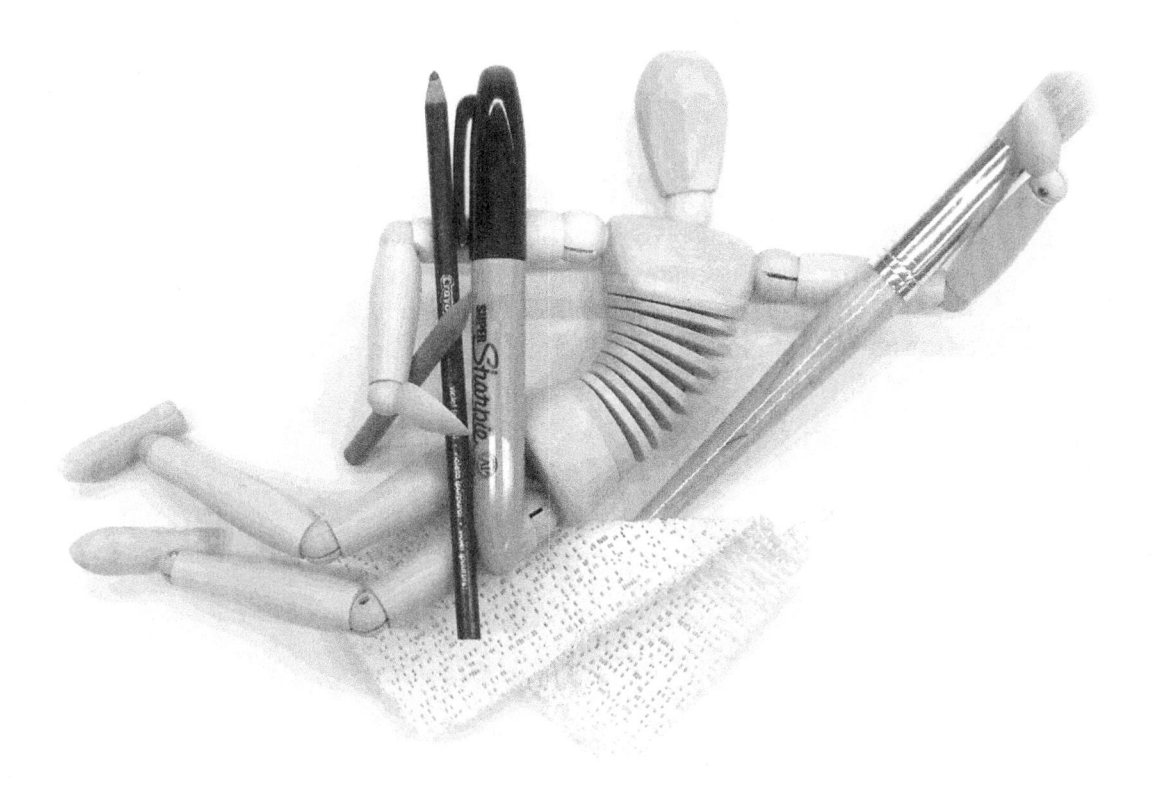

Your Name _____ Period _____

Class: _____

> You will use this ALL year!
> **DO NOT LOSE IT**

Student Edition

The Workbook For Art Students
A Classroom Companion for Painting, Drawing, and Sculpture

Fifth Edition, Soft Cover, Student Edition – 2025

Copyright 2021
By Eric Gibbons

Previously titled "The Art Student's Workbook."
All rights reserved. No part of this book may be used or reproduced by any means, graphic, electronic, or mechanical, including photocopying, recording, taping or by any information storage retrieval system without the written permission of the author except in the case of brief quotations embodied in critical articles and reviews.

ISBN: 1-940290-70-8
EAN-13: 978-1-940290-70-6

Printer: Amazon
Publisher: Firehouse Publishing

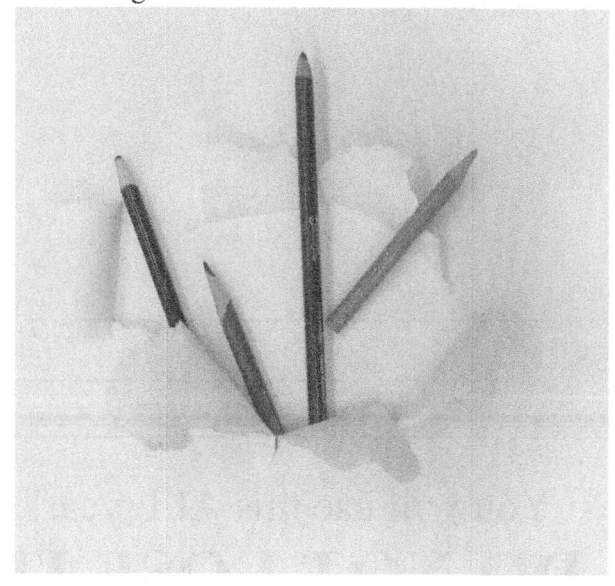

Student Workbook Contents

Rules & Expectations	4
First Survey	5
Elements of Art	7
Principles of Art	8
Color, Shape, & Expression	13
Material, Care, & Safety	22
Self-Expression	26
Printmaking & Vocabulary	44
Illustration	46
Math & Geometry in Art	54
Perspective & Shading	57
Human Proportions & Fashion	72
Science Concepts & Art	80
Engineering & Art	82
World Cultures & Diversity	84
English & Literature	92
Independent Projects	100
Art Quotes	108
Vocabulary & Reference	117
History & Research	123
Visual Analysis	152
Closure & Reflection	159
Video Notes	161
Sketchbook Ideas	174
Peer Project Reflections	180
Critique	189
Final Survey	194
Project Progress Sheets*	196+

*May be cut from the book and paired with projects.

Welcome to Art Class

BE ON TIME...
- It shows respect and responsibility!

STAY IN ASSIGNED SEATS...
- So you can be counted.
- So you don't distract others or yourself from work.
- So you don't get blamed for a mess by someone else at your assigned seat.
- So I can learn your name.

RESPECT:
- For each other
- For the teacher
- For our materials

STAY ON TASK...
- Part of your grade is that you are actively engaged in your work.
- Hard workers do not fail.
- Chatting is fine, but the work must get done.
- Keep your volume low.

FOLLOW DIRECTIONS...
- For safety, good grades, and so that our materials last a long time.

CLEAN UP AFTER YOURSELF...
- I am not your mother, nor your maid, and neither are your classmates.

COMPLETE YOUR WORK...
- A big part of your grade is project work, incomplete projects can make you fail.
- If you need more time, ask to borrow materials.
- Projects must be in before the close of the grades. After that, it's a zero.
- If you have been absent YOU need to find out what you missed.

STAY CREATIVE:
- Be as original as you can, don't copy other work or samples.
- Do your own work, but its okay to ask for a little help.

____% of your grade is based on project work
____% is based on assessments like tests/exams
____% is based on assessments like quizzes or class work
____% is based on your active participation
____% Other _____

Art Class First Survey:

First and last name printed _____ Period _____ - _____ Grade _____

Define Art: _____

_____

How many years of art class have you had before this class? _____

What do you feel your artistic ability is right now? 1 to 10 _____ (1 = NO ability at all, 10 = I'm pretty good at art.)

What do you hope we do in art before the end of the year? _____

_____

What would you like to get better at before the end of the year? _____

_____

Name some art elements (Line is one...) _____

_____

Name some art principles (Balance is one...) _____

_____

What is your favorite thing to draw, doodle, or make? _____

Even if it's not art related, what's your favorite hobby or "non-school activity" _____

_____

What are 4 words you would use to describe yourself _____, _____,

_____, _____, bonus word? _____

Sometimes schedules change at the beginning of the year, or you got a class you didn't expect and think you might want to change your schedule. Check off the statement you feel is true for you.

[__] I chose this class. [__] I did not choose this class so I might switch. [__] I will be switching out, 100%!

On the next page, draw the person sitting next to you. Their name is _____

Overview of 8 Art Elements https://bit.ly/AEpage7

A line is a _____ moving through _____. We can measure the _____ of a line and nothing else, therefore it is _____ dimensional or ___ -D.

A _____ that intersects itself will create a shape. A shape is _____ dimensional. There are _____ basic shapes. The one with the fewest number of sides is the _____. The one with the most sides is the _____.

A _____ that moves in _____ can create a form. There are ___ basic forms. The one with the fewest amount of sides is the _____, the one with the most sides is the _____.

There are ___ basic colors. Basic colors are also called _____ colors. When these basic colors mix they create _____ colors of which there are ____. Color is _____ light. Orange, red and yellow are considered _____ colors, while blue, green, and purple are considered _____ colors.

_____ refers to the weight of something; sometimes it is real and sometimes it is the way it looks. A _____ colored box will look heavier than a _____ colored one.

The roughness or smoothness of a surface refers to its _____. It can sometimes be made by repeating an art _____ many times.

All objects, art and non-art, take up _____. Many art elements move through it. This art element comes in 2 types, they are _____ meaning where the object IS, and _____, meaning where the object is NOT.

The art element of _____ helps us see all other art elements. We see everything because it is _____ off of an object or surface and back to our eye. When it is NOT bounced back to us we see _____.

Sometimes mass and light are combined and called _____. This is helpful when describing flat images that look 3D.

PRINCIPLES OF DESIGN WORKSHEET
Principles: https://bit.ly/APpage8

Define CONTRAST:

Give one example of this principle not in the book, so I know you understand it:

Define UNITY:

Give one example of this principle not in the book, so I know you understand it:

Define BALANCE:

Give one example of this principle not in the book, so I know you understand it:

Define EMPHASIS:

Give one example of this principle not in the book, so I know you understand it:

Define VARIETY:

Give one example of this principle not in the book, so I know you understand it:

(go to next page)

Define MOVEMENT:

Give one example of this principle not in the book, so I know you understand it:

Continued…

Define PATTERN:

Give one example of this principle not in the book, so I know you understand it:

What is a MOTIF?

What is the difference between CONTRAST and VARIETY?

Find any art image and list 3 art principles you can see in this artwork and how you know it to be true. Be specific so I know you understand it.

QUIZ

Art Elements

1. _____ is the simplest art element and is needed to draw anything.

2. _____ is the art element that is 2 dimensional. The basic ones are these three:

3. _____

4. _____

5. _____

6. _____ can sometimes be made by repeating an art element.

7. _____ helps things look 3D in a drawing or a painting.

8. _____ is reflected light. When we use a prism, we can see all of its components in white light.

9. _____ is a shape in 3-D or a 3 dimensional art element.

10. Draw and shade ALL the basic 3 dimensional "shapes" below.

Art Principles

1. _____ creates a sense of "sameness" to hold everything together visually.

2. _____ keeps things from getting too boring by adding visual differences.

3. _____ offers opposites to make the differences more obvious, even shocking sometimes.

4. _____ gives a sense of motion, either real or by design.

5. _____ makes a work feel settled, or complete on both the right and left in most cases. This principle is done in 2 ways, they are:

6. _____

7. _____

8. _____ is a repeated design. It can be natural or mechanical.

9. _____ makes one thing or area stand out more than the rest.

10. Illustrate & label one principle below.

Art Principles Worksheet   (tiny sketch below)

The artwork sample is called:

_____

by _____ .

It is from the _____
School of art. Please describe in FULL sentences
how you see the art principles used in his image.

Explain how the artist uses UNITY and where you see it used. Be Specific.

Explain how the artist uses CONTRAST and where you see it used. Be Specific.

Explain how the artist uses EMPHASIS and where you see it used. Be Specific.

Explain how the artist uses MOVEMENT and where you see it used. Be Specific.

Explain how the artist uses BALANCE and where you see it used. Be Specific.

Explain how the artist uses PATTERN and where you see it used. Be Specific.

Explain how the artist uses VARIETY and where you see it used. Be Specific.

Art Principles Worksheet

(tiny sketch below)

The artwork sample is called:

_____

by _____ .

It is from the _____
School of art. Please describe in FULL sentences
how you see the art principles used in his image.

Explain how the artist uses UNITY and where you see it used. Be Specific.

Explain how the artist uses CONTRAST and where you see it used. Be Specific.

Explain how the artist uses EMPHASIS and where you see it used. Be Specific.

Explain how the artist uses MOVEMENT and where you see it used. Be Specific.

Explain how the artist uses BALANCE and where you see it used. Be Specific.

Explain how the artist uses PATTERN and where you see it used. Be Specific.

Explain how the artist uses VARIETY and where you see it used. Be Specific.

Color Mixing

DIRECTIONS:
- **Using only primary colors, fill in this color wheel.**
- Put a "P" next to PRIMARY colors
- "S" next to secondary colors
- "W" next to warm colors
- "C" next to cool colors.
- "T" next to tertiary colors

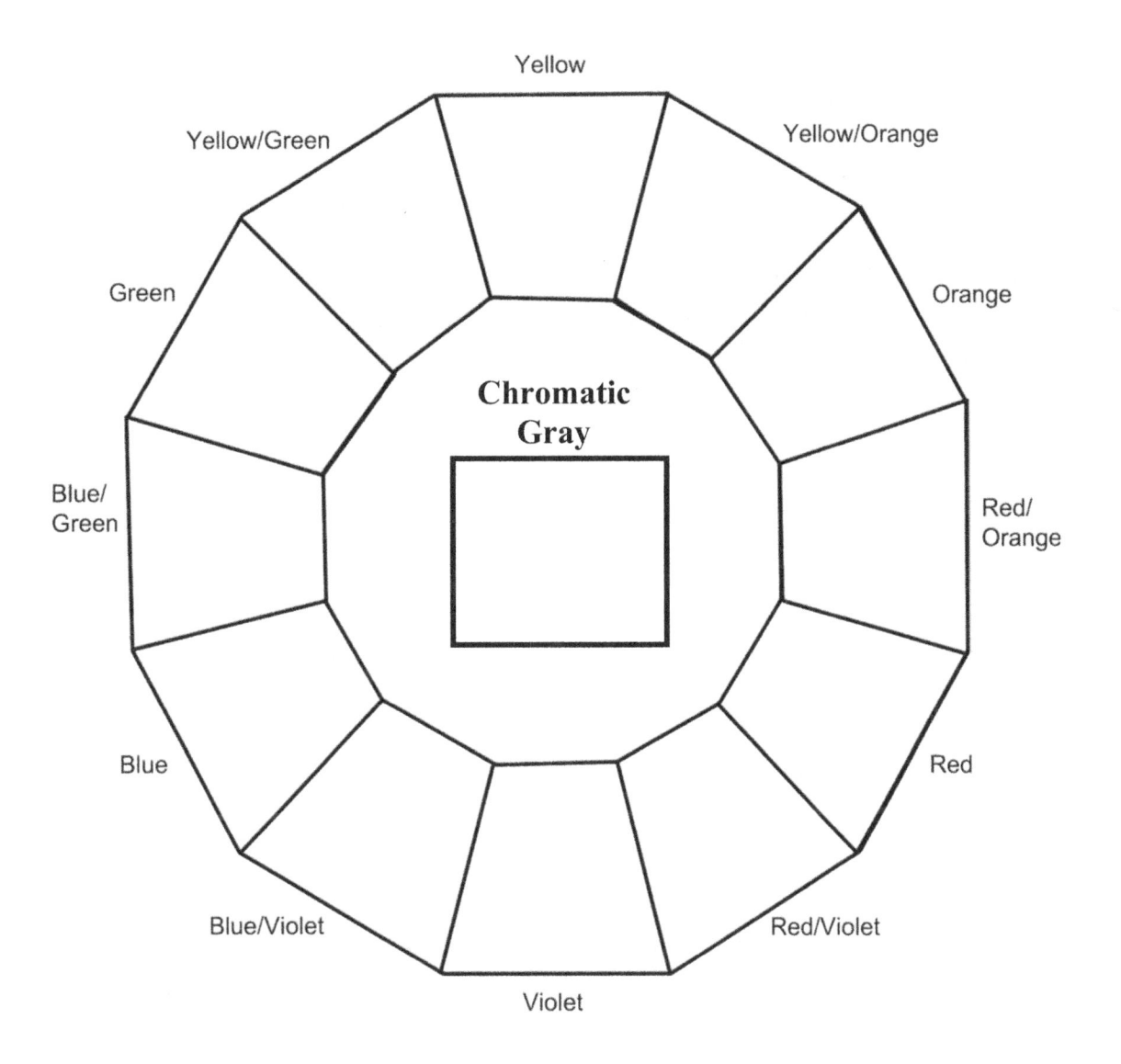

Yellow
Yellow/Orange
Yellow/Green
Orange
Green
Chromatic Gray
Blue/Green
Red/Orange
Blue
Red
Blue/Violet
Red/Violet
Violet

Tip: This can be done by layering primary colored pencils when coloring in. Use lightest colors first for best results... like yellow is lighter than blue.

Emotional Values of Shapes and Colors

△ Associations: _____

Emotional: _____

○ Associations: _____

Emotional: _____

☐ Associations: _____

Emotional: _____

Red: Associations: _____

Emotional: _____

Orange: Associations: _____

Emotional: _____

Yellow: Associations: _____

Emotional: _____

Green: Associations: _____

Emotional: _____

Blue: Associations: _____

Emotional: _____

Purple: Associations: _____

Emotional: _____

Black: Associations: _____

Emotional: _____

Brown: Associations: _____

Emotional: _____

White: Associations: _____

Emotional: _____

(Video Help at https://bit.ly/ShapesColors)

Draw combination of shapes to represent yourself. Then add color and pattern to express your personality.

Using the expressive information on the previous page, use color and shape to abstractly represent an important event in your life, positive or negative.

FAMILY

Describe 8 to 10 people in your family including yourself. Include both strengths and weaknesses. ALWAYS begin with people living in your household, and then extend that list into family not living with you. You may include people you knew who have died. **If you do not want to list names, use a nickname or initial so YOU know who you are writing about.** Create a mini sketch in the right margin below.

1. _____ : _____
   _____

2. _____ : _____
   _____

3. _____ : _____
   _____

4. _____ : _____
   _____

5. _____ : _____
   _____

6. _____ : _____
   _____

7. _____ : _____
   _____

8. _____ : _____
   _____

9. _____ : _____
   _____

10. _____ : _____
    _____

Sketch Page

Color Vocabulary

These are common vocabulary terms in art. Which ones do you already know? For others, use a resource, like "The Visual Experience" or another like the internet to write a definition for each vocabulary term.

Value: _____

Shading: _____

Chiaroscuro: _____

Spectrum: _____

Hue: _____

Primary Colors: _____

Secondary Colors: _____

Intermediate Colors: _____

Complementary Colors: _____

Triadic Colors: _____

Monochromatic Colors: _____

Intensity: _____

Color Harmonies: _____

Analogous Colors: _____

Warm Colors / Cool Colors: _____

COLOR WHEEL →

Use only the 3 primary colors to color in this diagram →

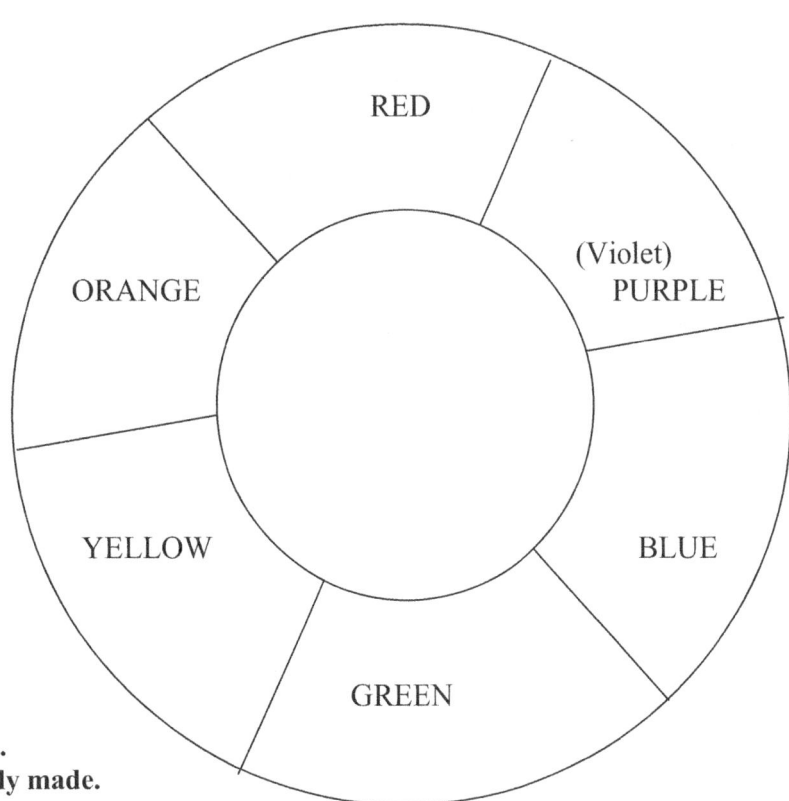

(Color wheel showing: RED, PURPLE (Violet), BLUE, GREEN, YELLOW, ORANGE)

Guess what the mix will be first...
Then try it and write what it really made.

Red + Blue = _____ (_____)

Blue + Yellow = _____ (_____)

Yellow + Red = _____ (_____)

Red + Blue + Yellow = _____ (_____)

Orange + Blue = _____ (_____)

Purple + Yellow = _____ (_____)

Green + Blue = _____ (_____)

Black + Yellow = _____ (_____)

Black + Yellow + Red = _____ (_____)

White + little Red + little Yellow + VERY little Black = _____ (_____)

Spectrum colors in order _____

Primary Color Practice:
Using only the primary colors, or CMY, do a drawing below and mix all your colors by overlapping them. Perhaps show shadows and highlights by pressing harder or softer.

Coloring Expectations

There is no reason to rush your work. We are more concerned with the process than what it looks like at the end. If the process is good then the product should be fine. When you rush things like coloring, it can damage the neatness and completeness portion of your grade. Though you may have been coloring for years, maybe since before you even came to school, there are a few things to keep in mind:

- You should use SMALL parallel strokes to color in
- The pressure you apply will determine the color intensity
- Try to stay within the boundaries you have set. (Stay in the lines)
- You should always color in layers. Nothing is the same color as a crayon
- Try shading with a neighboring or opposite color before choosing black
- Be patient, good work takes time

Though not every student is artistic, we expect all our students to strive to do their best. The back of this book has a color version of this expectation chart.

COLOR BIAS

In a perfect world Yellow and Red make Orange… and they do, sometimes.

Why not always??? Color is not perfect. It is made from minerals and chemicals and nothing in nature or on this earth is 100% perfect yellow. Some yellows are a bit orange, like a bright sunny yellow, and some are a bit green like lemon yellow.

ALL colors "**LEAN**" a bit one way or another. This is called **Color Bias**. Some companies even label their paint so you can see which way the color "leans." When mixing colors, you need to choose colors that "lean" towards each other. If you do not, your colors will be less bright and even brown-ish. (This might be a good thing when painting natural elements like dirt, grass, bark, rocks etc…)

Color bias can work for you or against you, but you need to use it to your advantage.

<u>**AVOID BLACK**</u> in your paintings of nature. It is better to mix color opposites or compliments to make a dark tone. There is very little black in nature. Burnt wood/charcoal is black, some deep dark shadows may need black, but 90% of the time black should be avoided. It is often the easiest way a professional can spot amateur work. Black kills color and only in a few instances is this a good thing.

<u>Mixing Watercolors:</u> The lids of most watercolor sets are detachable for a reason… you can mix colors on the lid, but separate it to clean it. HOWEVER when painting a landscape, SOMETIMES it's better to mix right on the paper so the color is uneven. Nature is organic and does not have perfect colors. Imperfections in your paint mixtures might be a desirable effect.

Paint Brush Care

Paint brushes are an important tool in an artist's toolbox. They are expensive and need to be cared for properly. Some paints, like acrylics, can ruin brushes if they are not cleaned properly.

- Always use COLD water to clean a brush. Hot water melts the glue that holds the brush together
- Be sure to wash the collar of the brush too
- Test your clean brush on paper before storing
- Store brushes with the brush-end-up

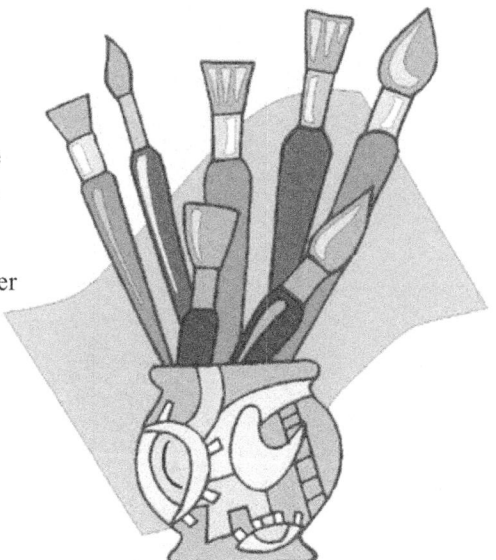

BRUSH   COLLAR   HANDLE

PLASTER WORK

Plaster is activated by water. It is important to be aware of how you set up your area for plaster work.

1. Cover your table area with paper or plastic. Remove jewelry.

2. Keep plaster and water far enough away that the water won't accidently splash, drip, or spill on the plaster.

3. Be sure others near you won't interfere with your set-up or cause an accident as well. Several people can work from one bucket.

Once plaster has been dipped in water, it must be strained through the fingers and applied to your base or object to be covered. Plaster will need to be 2 or 3 layers thick to be strong.

If you accidently get water on a plaster strip, use it immediately.

Plaster cannot be re-used once it has hardened.

Smooth strips with your hands as you apply them. Without smoothing, one layer will not bond with the last.

NEVER put plaster down a sink. Not from your hands, not from the bucket. It will form stones in the pipes and be VERY expensive to repair.
- Wash hands in plaster water first
- Stir plaster in bucket with hands and dump in to grass or dumpster
- Let bucket dry and crack plaster into garbage

Though plaster will come out of clothes, you may find wearing a smock is good protection. Tutorial: https://youtu.be/2_6pnuteHtE

Liquid Plaster

Plaster is activated by water. It is important to be aware of how you set up your area for plaster work.

1. Cover your table area with paper or plastic. Remove jewelry.

2. Keep plaster and water far enough away that the water won't accidently splash, drip, or spill on the plaster.

3. Be sure others near you won't interfere with your set-up by accident as well. Several people can work from one bucket.

Determine how much liquid plaster you need (cup or bucket). Use LESS THAN HALF that amount of water.

Hot water hardens plaster faster than cold water; choose accordingly.

Add dry plaster with a cup or scoop or spoon by sprinkling a little at a time. Too much at once will ruin your plaster mixture. Be sure to sprinkle evenly all around your container so it fills evenly. DO NOT STIR THE MIXTURE!

Slowly add plaster until it forms islands in the water that do not go below the surface of the water. See picture above.

Once you have sufficient islands, you may stir. The more you stir the faster the plaster will harden. *(FYI: Plaster heats up as it dries; use caution if applying to body)*

NEVER put plaster down a sink. Not from your hands, not from the bucket. It will form stones in the pipes and be VERY expensive to repair.
- Wash hands in plaster water first
- Let bucket dry and crack plaster into the garbage. Toss cups.

Hint: *Acrylic paint or acrylic medium can be added to plaster. Acrylics make the plaster dry mush more slowly. Add 1/10 of acrylic medium to the water **before** adding plaster.*

Tutorial: https://youtu.be/RnG4X-bFUgs

Razor Blades SAFETY

Tutorial: https://youtu.be/lgnfE0E2GrI

ALWAYS get permission to use any sharp tools.
- NEVER play with these tools.
- Taking one out of the classroom is ILLEGAL and considered a weapon in school.
- Check that the blade is secure and tight.
- Keep it capped when not in use.
- Protect table when cutting.
- ALWAYS cut away from fingers or body.
- Hold like a pencil for best control.

IF YOU GET A CUT…
- Hold cut tightly closed.
- Tell teacher immediately.
- Wash with running water.
- Pinch closed with paper towel.
- See teacher for band-aid or hall pass to the nurse.

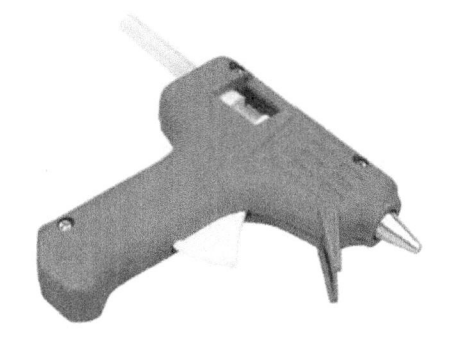

GLUE GUN SAFETY

GLUE GUNS can heat up to about 400 degrees. They will burn deeply.
NEVER touch the tip of a glue gun. EVEN the glue that comes out can burn badly. Use a craft-stick to move the glue if you need to. Glue guns stay hot for a while after being unplugged! A glue gun is NOT A TOY!

IF YOU GET BURNED, go to the sink quickly and rinse with cool water. If you get a blister, get a pass to the nurse.

Goals

What are some life goals you have? Things you hope to achieve in the future.

- By the time I graduate from high school, I hope to have :

- In 10 years I hope I have :

- In 20 or 30 years I hope I have :

- Before I die, I hope that I have :

List some things that can hold you back from reaching your goals:

1.

2.

3.

4.

5.

6.

Sketch Page

The Story of My Life

- First time to drive
- First hunting trip
- The time you won an award
- First time you caught your parents lying
- First time you went to a funeral
- Birth of a new family member
- First job, or interview, or first firing
- A time you were betrayed
- A time you got your first paycheck
- First trip outside the USA
- A time you had to move
- A time you saved someone's life or someone saved yours.
- First time you were tempted to do something wrong.

What are your 4 or 5 life changing or important events:

1_____

2_____

3_____

4_____

5_____

We say "don't judge a book by its cover" but we all have a cover, an outer appearance that others see and make assumptions about. These assumptions may or may not be true. If you had to create a cover for the book of YOUR LIFE, what might it look like?

Please research some examples of "Altered Books" and sketch or write down some ideas you think you might be able to use.

Sketch Page

9 Important Things

What are the 9 most important things to you? They can be real things like a dog or a person, or a feeling like love, or freedom. What are the 9 things you do not want to live without? Write each one in a box below, and draw a simple symbol for each. If nature was important to you, you could draw a leaf.

Hands

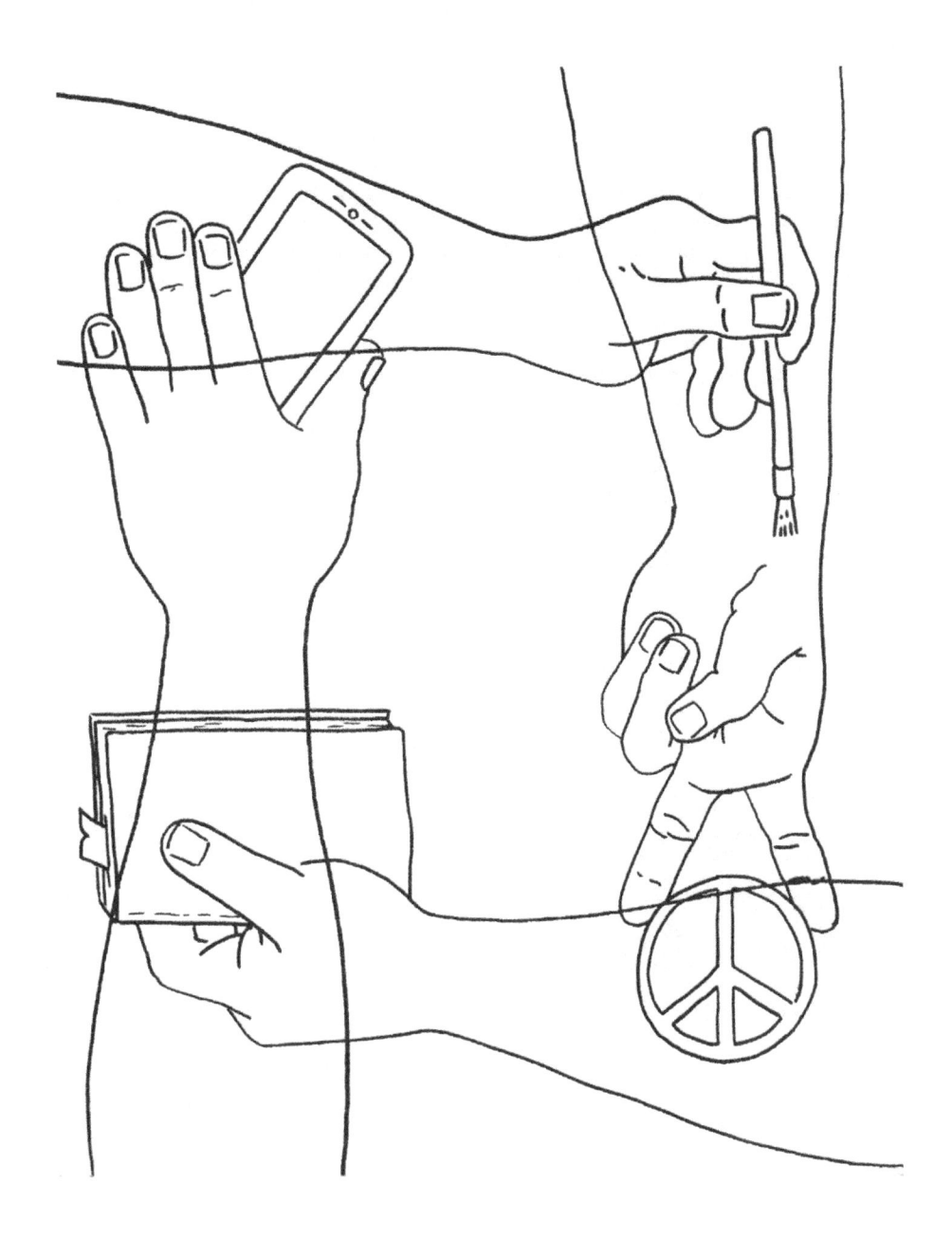

Hands We use objects and symbols every day. Trace your hands 4 times, overlapping, then go back in and fill in simple details like nails and main wrinkles. Be sure to include 4 important symbols that relate to you or the things you value.

Consider what you will put in the center. Will you overlap letters of your name, create a single important symbol or do a self portrait? It's up to you.

Where lines overlap making new shapes, color in each shape a different color. This is a great time to learn to blend colors. Try using only primary colors and have white available as a bonus color. Because our lines are black, black color is not an option for this project.

Masks

Masks are usually used to hide the identity of the wearer. However, in this project, we are going to design a mask that will show others a side of you that you normally keep hidden from others, or something people don't normally know about you. This can be done through using symbols and shapes that you can either paint on the mask, or shape the mask to look like. So, if people assume you are kind of "ditzy" but you're really smart, you can shape the mask into the shape of an owl to represent how smart you are.

1. Sketch out how you want your mask to look including any symbols that you might paint on to the mask. Also, write down the meaning of your symbols as a reminder for yourself if you have a number of symbols that you are painting unto the mask.

> REMEMBER: This can be a mask that can be worn OR a mask that is simply decoration on a wall. You should decide what kind it will be before you begin , so you'll know how to build it.

2. We will create a foam base and build up the features on the face. Aluminum foil works too. WARNING: Carving foam is VERY messy. So is plaster work. YOU are responsible for YOUR area. No one will be allowed to sit in alternative seats for this project. If someone irresponsible sits near you… you may become responsible for their mess in your space.

3. After carving the foam, you'll plaster it. After it dries, you can begin to paint and add materials like feathers or other objects to the mask. You may want to bring some craft items from home if you do not have them here.

Sketch Page

Who Am I?

Often outward perceptions are different from reality. For example, people may know you like art, but may not know you traveled internationally. You may use visual codes to hide information you do not really want to share with others. We will use these lists to come up with an expressive work of art.

What I know about myself	**How the world sees me <u>or</u> how I see the world, <u>or</u> how I see my future.**
1. _____	1. _____
2. _____	2. _____
3. _____	3. _____
4. _____	4. _____
5. _____	5. _____
6. _____	6. _____
7. _____	7. _____
8. _____	8. _____
9. _____	9. _____
10. _____	10. _____
11. _____	11. _____
12. _____	12. _____

How might you use art to express what you have written about above? Could it be an altered book with one kind of cover and different inside pages? Perhaps a silhouette with what you know about yourself inside and the other list on the outside... Maybe a box showing the differences inside and out. Start with a sketch on the next page for ideas.

Sketch Page

Memorial Project

We will be creating an artwork based on someone special to you who is *no longer around you*. This could be through a death, but also because they may have moved, lost contact, or a separation because of a divorce. If you have not lost someone in your life, please pick someone you admire who is not living.

For privacy, if you prefer, you may use the person's initials to write below. Their name is: _____

Write about your most vivid memory of this person.

_____
_____
_____
_____

What about him or her has changed your life?

_____
_____
_____

If you could tell people only one thing about this person, what would you say?

_____
_____

Please write 5 positive words describing the person.

_____

Did he or she have any shortcomings, negative traits? Mention 1 or 2 of them.

_____

Sketch Page

Exploration of Culture:

What is *Culture*? The customs, arts, social institutions, and heritage of a particular nation, people, or other social group. What is/are your cultures?

_____,__ _____, _____, _____

Artists like Romare Bearden and others often tie their culture into their artwork to connect to a larger community.

- Write about an event that shaped who you are: positive or negative?
- What do you celebrate culturally, as part of a larger community?
- Part of being _____ means _____.
- The best part of being _____ is _____.
- _____ is a cultural hero for _____ because _____.

_____

_____

_____

_____

_____

_____

_____

Sketch on the next page a scene that helps illustrate some or all of your writing.

Sketch Page

Idiom Project

An idiom is a phrase, when taken as a whole, has a meaning different from the meanings of the individual words. Idioms can be cultural or specific to a language or community. The phrase *"raining cats and dogs"* is an example of an idiom. English speakers understand that this doesn't refer to domesticated animals at all, but that it describes very intense rain.

Based on your own cultural background(s), look up 3 idioms and record them below. Pick one to illustrate on the next page.

Culture: _____

Idiom: _____
_____
_____

Translation: _____
_____

Culture: _____

Idiom: _____
_____
_____

Translation: _____
_____

Culture: _____

Idiom: _____
_____
_____

Translation: _____
_____

Unsung Heroes

1. Five richest people in the world.
   a. _____
   b. _____
   c. _____
   d. _____
   e. _____
2. Five sports trophy winners.
   a. _____
   b. _____
   c. _____
   d. _____
   e. _____
3. Last five winners of Miss America.
   a. _____
   b. _____
   c. _____
   d. _____
   e. _____
4. 5 people who have won the Nobel prize.
   a. _____
   b. _____
   c. _____
   d. _____
   e. _____
5. Five Academy Award winners.
   a. _____
   b. _____
   c. _____
   d. _____
   e. _____

1. 5 teachers who were good to you.
   a. _____
   b. _____
   c. _____
   d. _____
   e. _____
2. 5 people who have helped you through a difficult time.
   a. _____
   b. _____
   c. _____
   d. _____
   e. _____
3. 5 people you would share your lottery winnings with.
   a. _____
   b. _____
   c. _____
   d. _____
   e. _____
4. 5 people you miss in your life.
   a. _____
   b. _____
   c. _____
   d. _____
   e. _____
5. 5 of the kindest people you know.
   a. _____
   b. _____
   c. _____
   d. _____
   e. _____

Which list was easier to create? _____

Who appears on your lists the most? _____

Why are they so special to you? _____

_____

_____

What kind of artwork could you make to honor that person's influence?

Printmaking Experience

1. What kind of printmaking did you explore?
_____
_____

2. Describe the process:
_____
_____
_____
_____
_____

3. Name a famous artist who also did this.
_____

4. What was most challenging for you?
_____
_____
_____

5. What was most successful for you?
_____
_____
_____

Printmaking Vocabulary

1. Brayer: A small, hand-held rubber roller used to spread printing ink evenly on a surface before printing.

2. Block/Plate: A piece flat material, with a design on its surface, used to print repeated impressions of that design. Called a PLATE in etching and engraving.

3. Printmaking: The process of designing and producing prints using a printing block, woodcut, etching, screen-printing, etc.

4. Edition: A set of identical/similar prints, that are numbered and signed. This set of prints have been pulled by or under the supervision of the artist.

5. Registration: Adjustment of separate plates/blocks, or paper in color printing to ensure correct alignment of the colors.

6. Burnishing: Rubbing the back of printing paper on an inked block/plate to make a print.

7. Monoprint: A print made as an edition of one. It is an image painted on glass or plexi-glass, and transferred (or stamped) onto paper. Each single print is unique.

8. Printing Press: A device used by a fine art printmaker to produce prints one copy at a time. It applies pressure between a sheet of paper and an inked printing plate.

9. Proof: Trial prints done to check the status of the work.

10. Prints: A process to transfer an image to another surface. Copies of an original artwork.

Sketch Page

Music

1. My favorite song right now is _____ by _____

2. I like it so much because
_____

_____

Music can "speak' to us, just as art can. Music can stir emotions of all kinds from joy, and excitement, to sadness, and pain, to even emotions of anger and inspiring people to take action!

3. A song that I like, that might surprise people is : _____ by _____

4. It reminds me of _____

_____

5. A song that makes me feel sad is : _____ by _____

6. It reminds me of _____

_____

7. A song that I like that gives me hope or joy is : _____ by _____

8. This is because: _____

_____

Highlight the one above you feel has the most visual imagery. (Like you could *draw* it.)

Find the lyrics of the song on an iPad or your phone, and write just 1 paragraph from the song below. If the song includes words that are inappropriate for school, add a black space.

_____

_____

_____

_____

_____

Sketch Page

Alphabet Themes

LIST 5 themes for yourself and 3 themes of those close to you (Mom, Dad...)
BROAD themes are better than focused ones. You will have more choices.
For instance, choosing *Field Hockey* limits the amount of imagery you can use, but if your theme was *Sports* then you would have tons of other stuff to incorporate.

- Instead of Clothes, choose fashion (Then you can include Fashion Logos)
- Instead of Vegetables, choose Foods
- Instead of Rock and Roll, choose Music

There are 3 levels of difficulty to this project.

Level 1: A Single object repeated to create a whole alphabet, like the balloons below. If done very well can get a high potential grade of a low "A."

Level 2: A single concept with 30% to 60% related original ideas thrown in, like a theme of Plants. If done very well can get a high potential grade of a mid-range "A."

Level 3: Every letter is a different image within the theme. This is the most difficult and potentially can get the highest grade of 100%. (Here is a Logo Alphabet)

The Letters do not have to coordinate with the meaning. "A" does not have to be "APPLE" the symbol just has to be an "A" SHAPE.

Helpful Hints

DO NOT START WITH "A"

Start with the easiest ideas and cross them off. If you chose SPORTS, make a ball and cross off the "O" first! Use the alphabet below to cross off what you have sketched.

REMEMBER! Letters can look many different ways and still be that letter.

$$A a A a A A a$$

Cross off letters as you sketch them.

$$A B C D E F G H$$
$$I J K L M N O$$
$$P Q R S T U$$
$$V W X Y Z$$

What is your theme? _____

Alphabet Sketch Page

Name Project Worksheet

My favorite Foods.

_____

_____

_____

_____

My hobbies or sports.

_____

_____

_____

_____

Where have I been on vacation before?

_____

_____

_____

_____

Pets I have had.

_____

_____

_____

Favorite songs of musicians.

_____

_____

_____

Stuff I collect.

_____

_____

_____

_____

My favorite holiday(s).

_____

_____

What I would buy if I won the lottery.

_____

_____

_____

_____

What makes me unique?

_____

_____

_____

_____

Can you use the information from this worksheet to illustrate your name?

Languages that don't look like English @ Translate.google.com

Amharic	**Kurdish** (Sorani)	**Sinhala**
Arabic	**Kyrgyz**	**Tajik**
Armenian	**Macedonian**	**Tamil**
Assamese	**Maithili**	**Tatar**
Belarusian	**Malayalam**	**Telugu**
Bengali	**Marathi**	**Thai**
Bhojpuri	**Meiteilon**	**Tigrinya**
Chinese (either style)	**Mongolian**	**Ukrainian**
Dhivehi	**Myanmar** (Burmese)	**Urdu**
Dogri	**Nepali**	**Yiddish**
Greek	**Odia (Oriya)**	
Gujarati	**Pashto**	
Hebrew	**Persian**	
Hindi	**Punjabi**	
Japanese	**Quechua**	
Kannada	**Russian**	
Kazakh	**Sanskrit**	
Khmer	**Serbian**	
Korean	**Sindhi**	

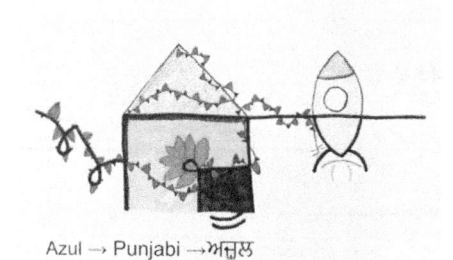

Eric → Chinese → 埃里克

Azul → Punjabi → ਅਜ਼ੁਲ

Promise → Armenian → խոստում

52

Sketch Page

Grids

Grids can be a great way to transform a design, enlarge or reduce a drawing. They are often used to make murals. Tutorial: https://youtu.be/eTfSt7HYYXg

The following pages have 2 grids of different scale. You can place a piece of plastic, acetate, or overhead sheet on top of the grid and trace the lines using a ruler and sharpie marker to have your own grid. It can be placed over a photograph, magazine image, etc, and transferred to a similar grid on another paper.

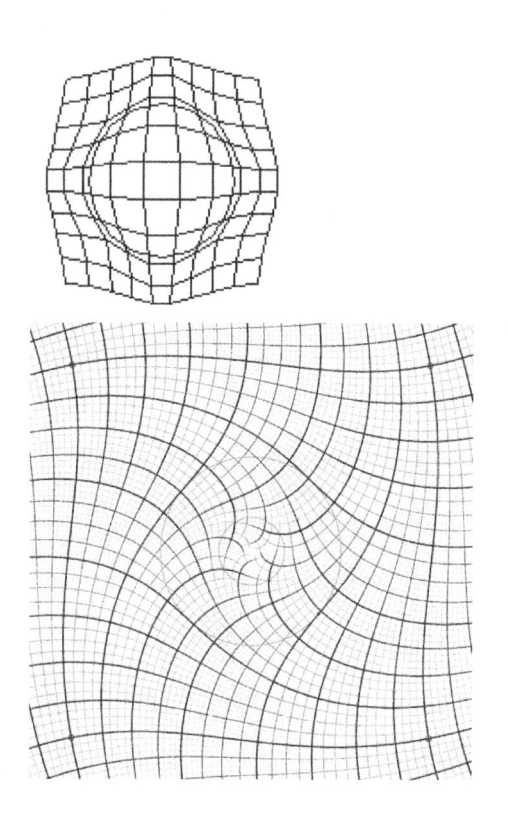

Sometimes it is fun to create a *"warped"* grid that has waves in it and curves and transfer the design into it to create a surrealistic or altered transfer.

When doing a warped grid, put a regular grid on top of an image, and then create a warped grid the image will be transferred to.

With the warped grid, straight lines are not necessary. It is sometimes best to make the outside border and divide that shape in half, and each subsequent division in half again until the grid has the number of divisions you feel will work. This can be done by hand with visual estimates.

Tutorial: https://youtu.be/fqIhUZ0seX8

Take your time and go square-by-square to transfer your design.

The regular gridding technique is very old and we know it was used by many Renaissance artists like Leonardo da Vinci.

Perspective

(1 Point, 2 Point, and 3 Point)

Vocabulary

- Perspective

- Horizon

- Vanishing Point

- Parallel

- Converging

- Vertical

- Eye Level

This is an example of 1 Point Perspective. Everything seems to be going to one point "A".

Your Name in 1 Point Perspective

1. Can you draw your name with block letters? Do it below.
2. Create a horizon and vanishing point.
3. Make all corners of your name go to that vanishing point.
4. DO NOT draw lines that overlap the letters of your name.

Use a ruler and draw along all the edges that go into the background. Where do they meet? What do we call this point? Is it the same for the image below?

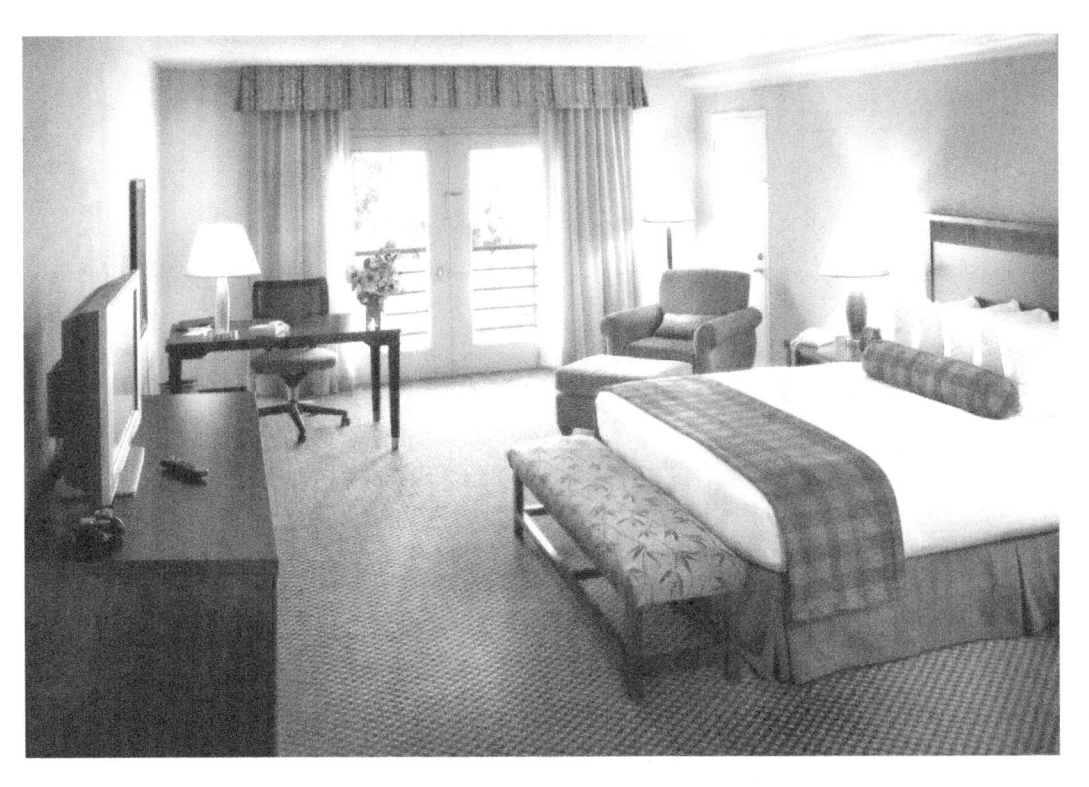

Surreal school drawing samples in 1 Point Perspective.

By Ryan Orlofsky

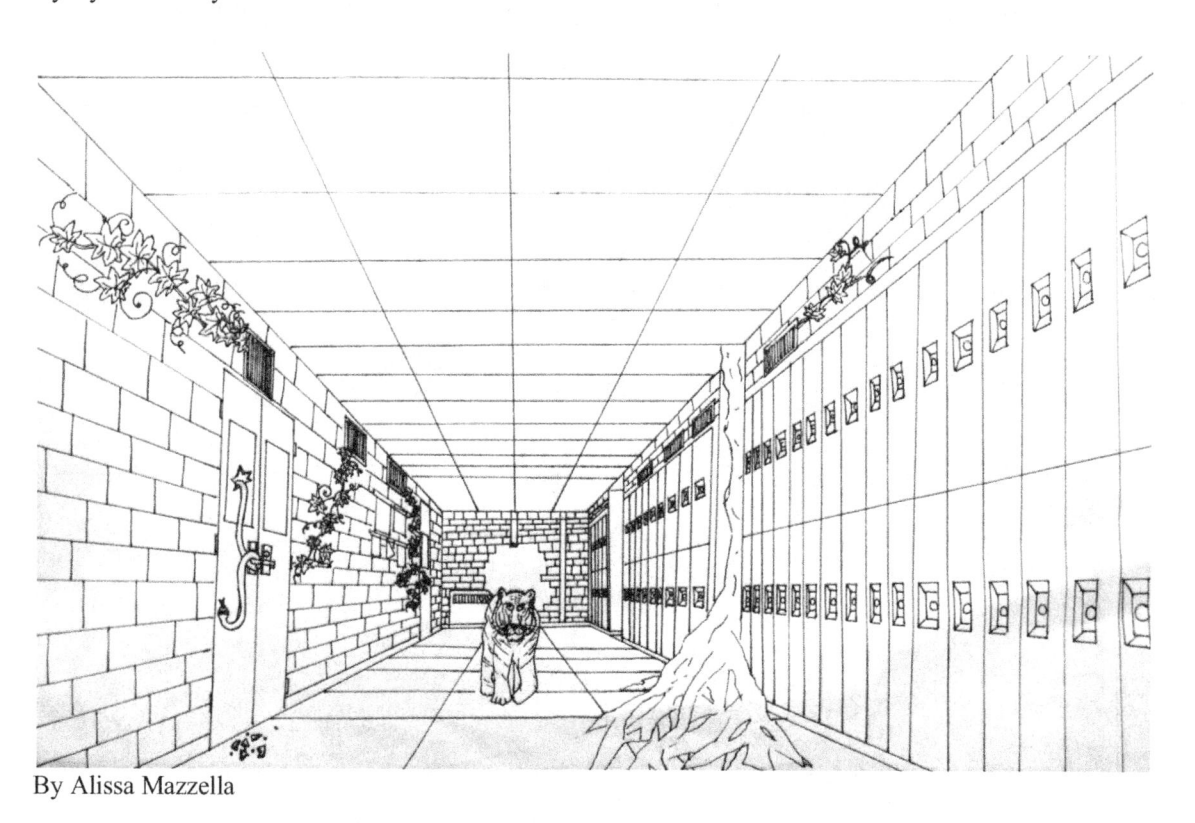

By Alissa Mazzella

This is an example of 2 Point Perspective. See how both sides seem to converge to different points on the same horizon.

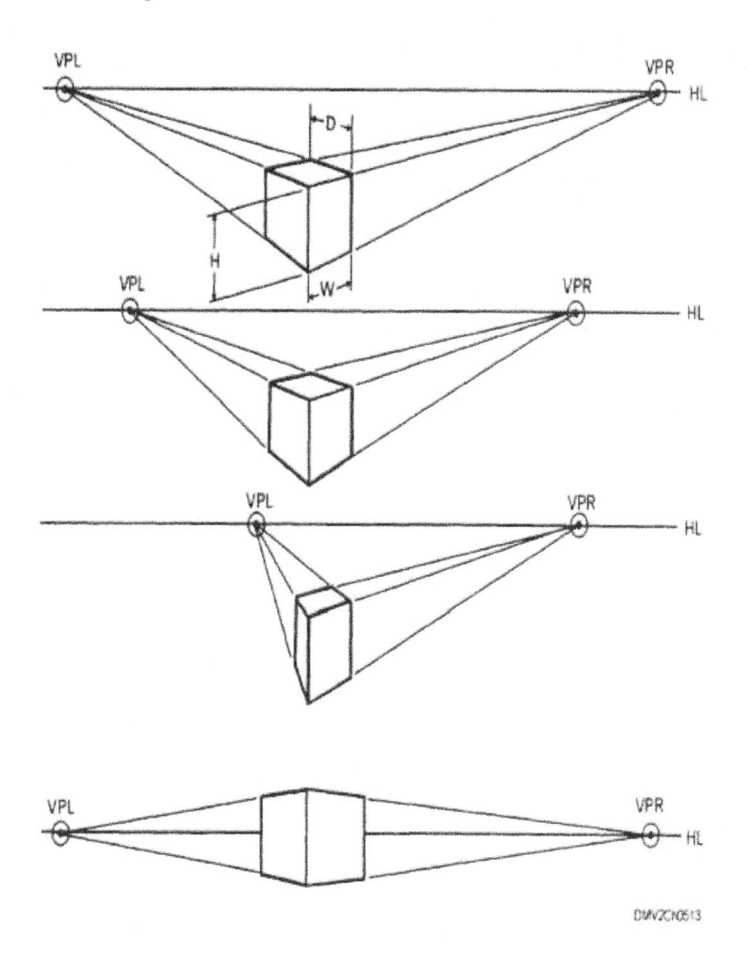

This is how 2 point perspective is used to draw boxes. You may not be required to do a 2 point perspective drawing, but you need to know about it and explain the concept.

THREE-POINT PERSPECTIVE

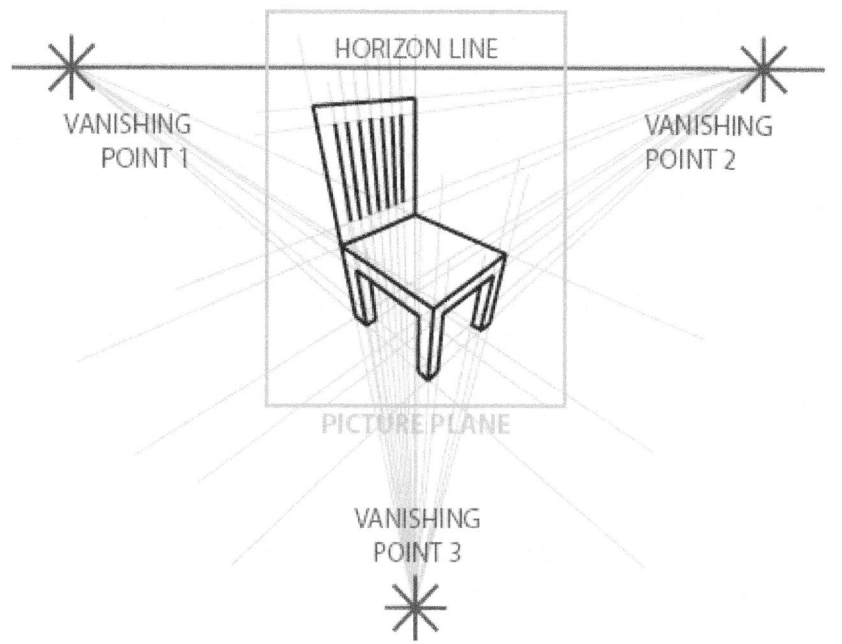

3 Point Perspective is shown above. It is NOT a requirement to do a project in 3 point perspective, but you do need to understand the concept.

Try to draw a cube below and make it look 3-D.

Drawing Boxes in 1 point perspective

1. Draw a horizontal line with a ruler, somewhere below. This is the *Horizon*. (It can cut through a box)
2. Draw a **dot** somewhere on the line.
3. Make the corners of the squares below connect to that **dot,** we'll call that the *Vanishing Point*.
4. Erase completely any lines that cut through a square.
5. Use parallel lines to show the back edge of each box.
6. Erase lines that go beyond the end of each box.

Can you find the vanishing point in these 2 images?

Perspective Practice 1

Perspective Practice 2

Crosshatching

Wood Composition. Forms representing circle of friends

Repeated lines can create the illusion of shadow and form. The above image was done step by step to the right. This is the same technique used to create the faces you see on a dollar bill.

It can be done also with dots (Stippling) or any repeated line, even scribbles.

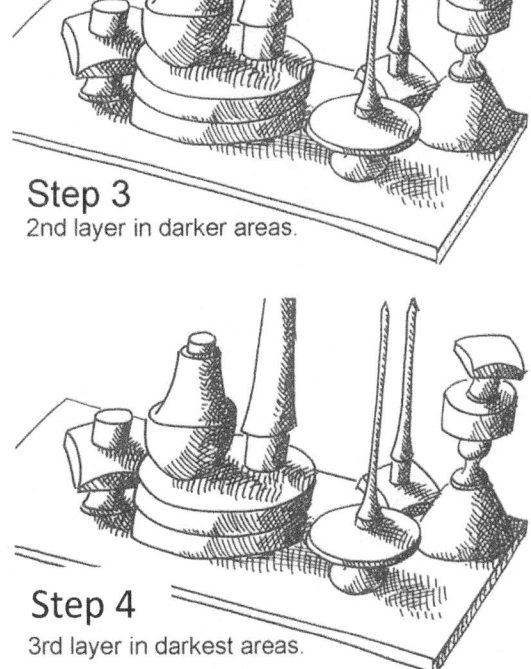

Step 1
Linear Drawing

Step 2
One layer of hatching all shaded areas

Step 3
2nd layer in darker areas.

Step 4
3rd layer in darkest areas.

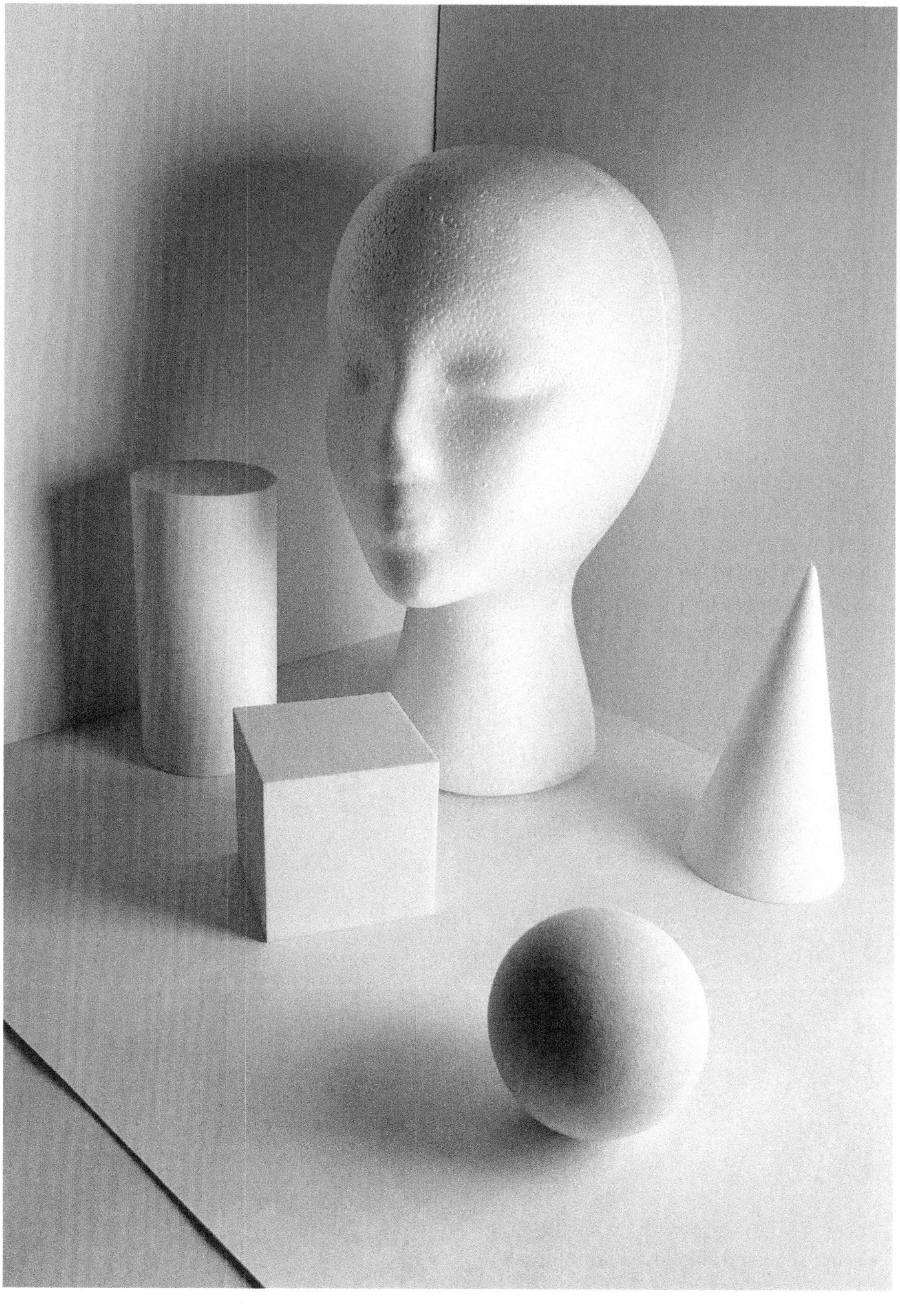

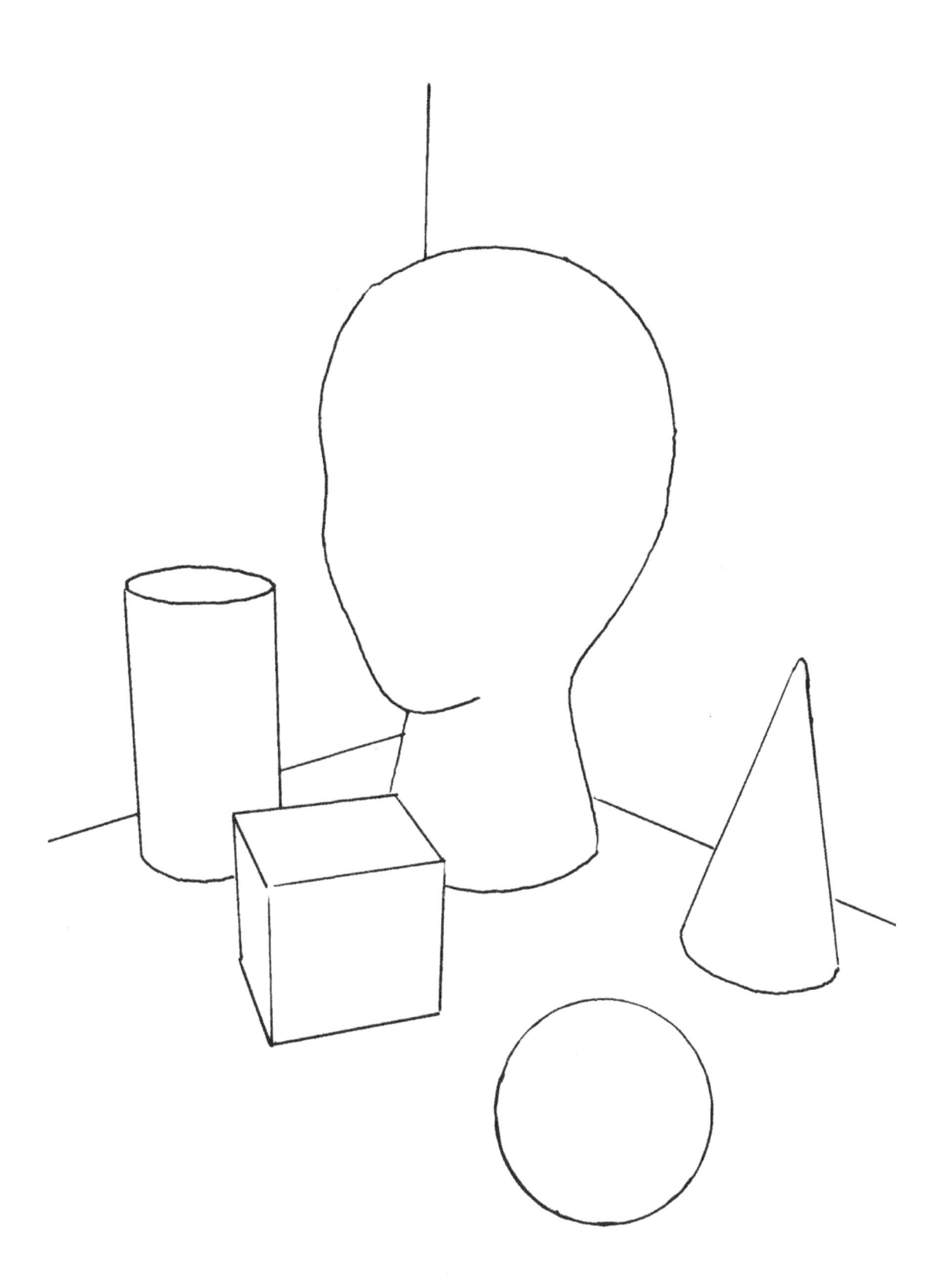

Practice your shading technique(s) above based on the photo on the left.

Coloring Spheres

This first example is monochromatic (variation of a single color, like black or blue...)

MONOCHROMATIC

Please color in the following 6 circles. See the sample so your circles look like shaded spheres too.

- Primary colors
- Secondary colors
- Analogous colors
- Complementary colors
- Any color plus black and white
- 1 color; use pressure to show light and dark.

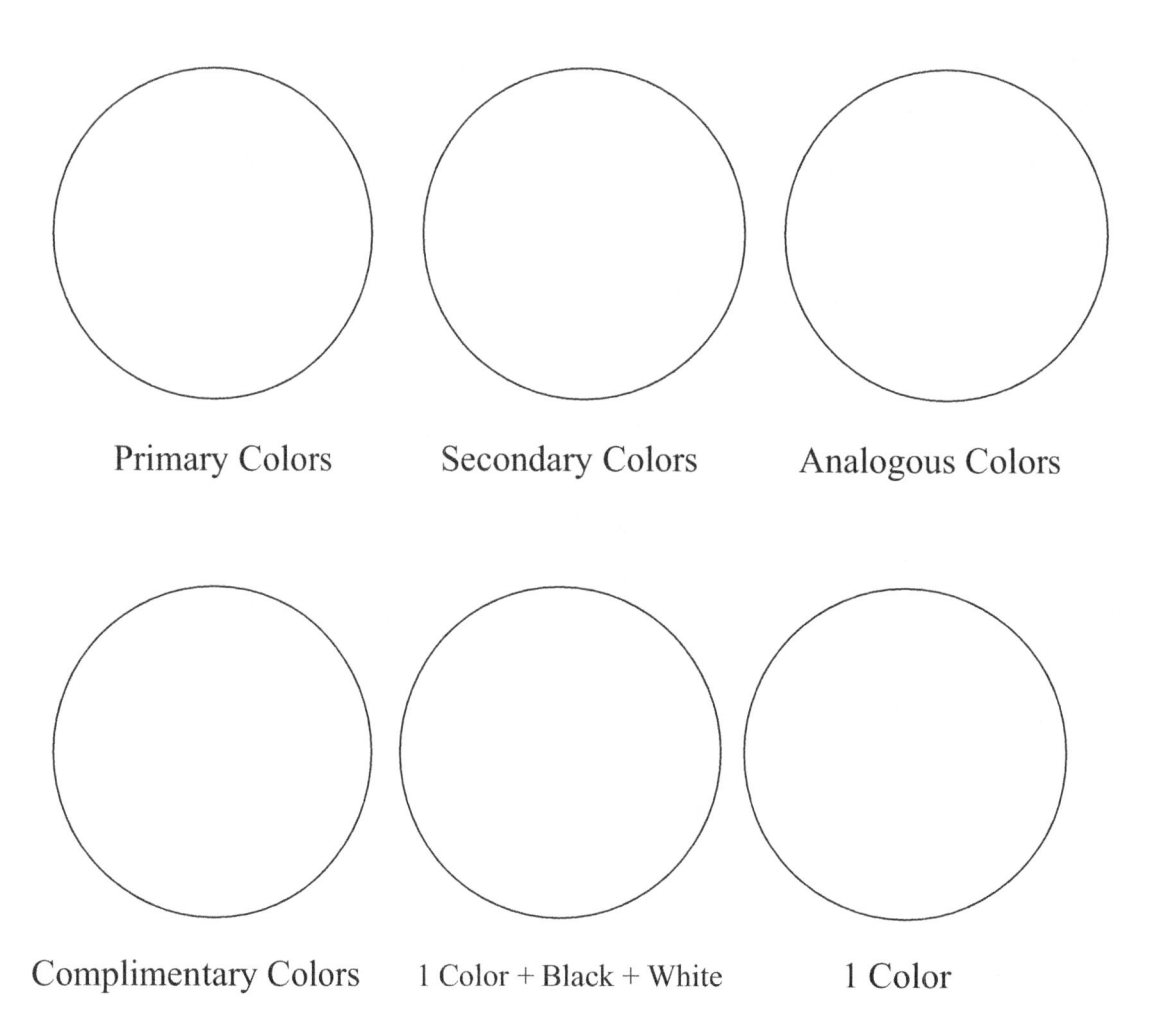

Primary Colors   Secondary Colors   Analogous Colors

Complimentary Colors   1 Color + Black + White   1 Color

4 Basic Forms

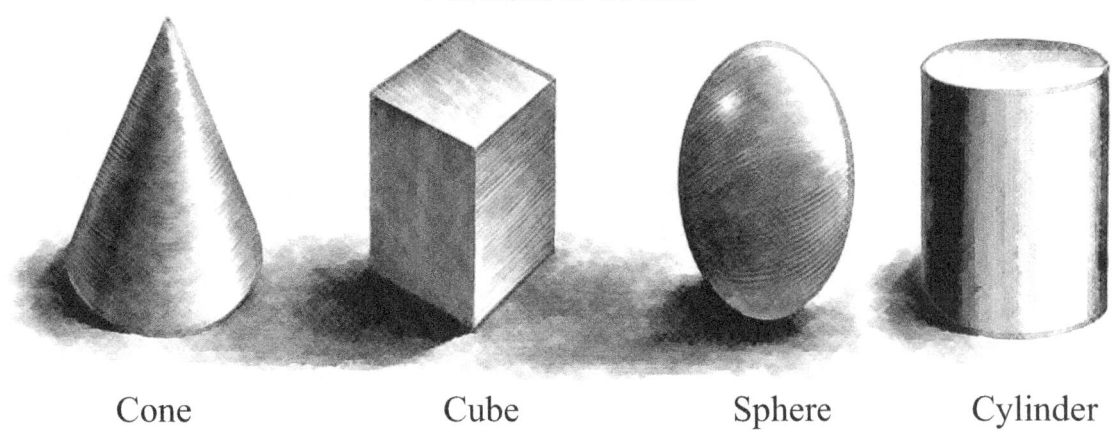

Cone   Cube   Sphere   Cylinder

Try drawing the 4 forms here. Color and shade them.

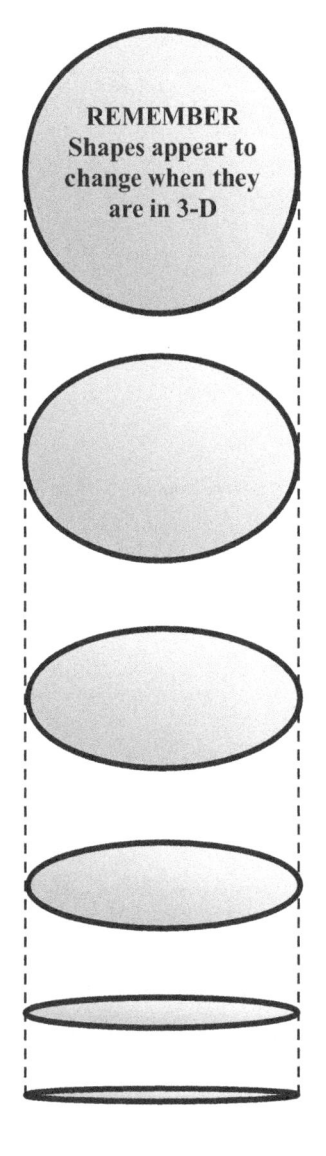

REMEMBER
Shapes appear to change when they are in 3-D

Face Proportions

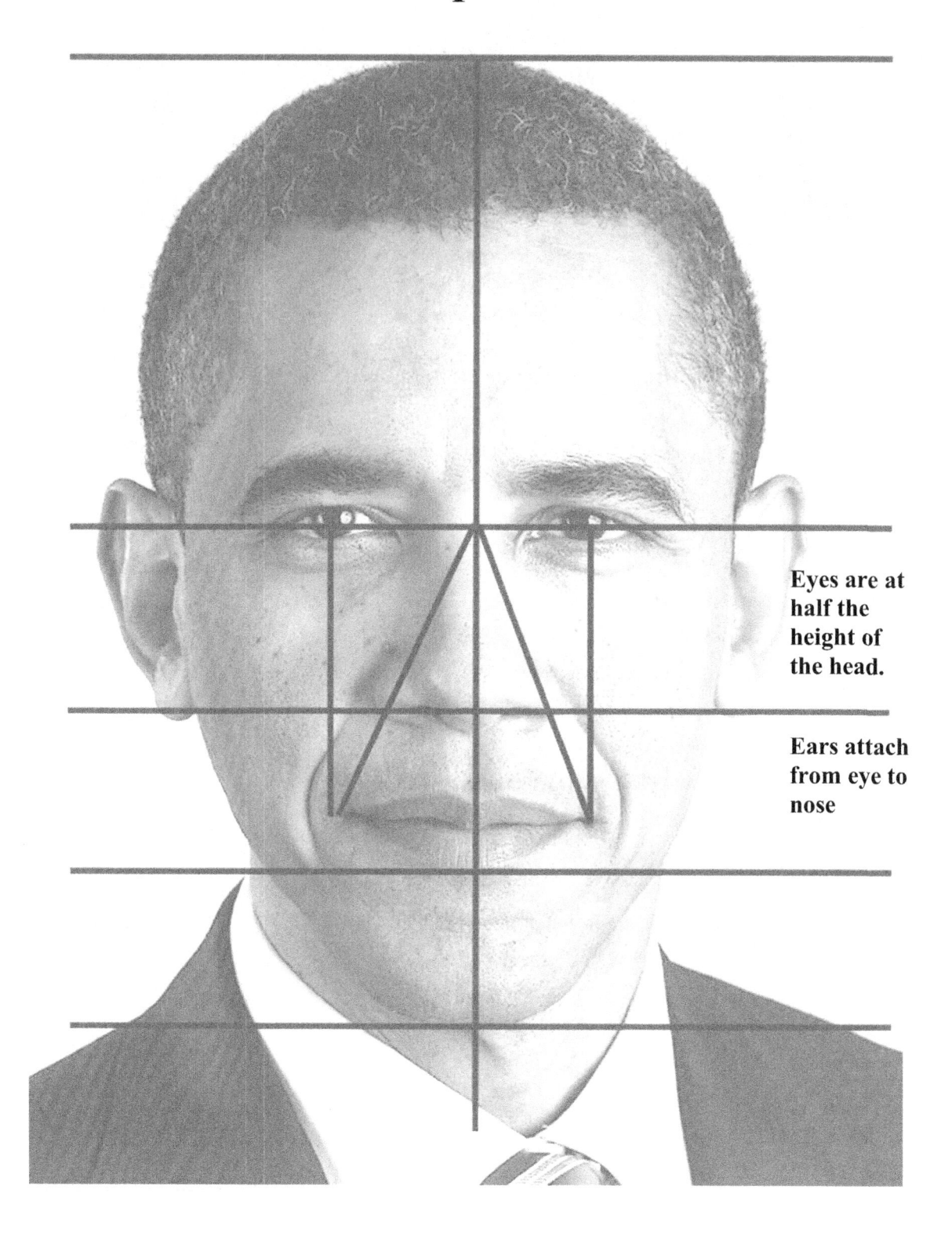

Eyes are at half the height of the head.

Ears attach from eye to nose

Face Map Proportions

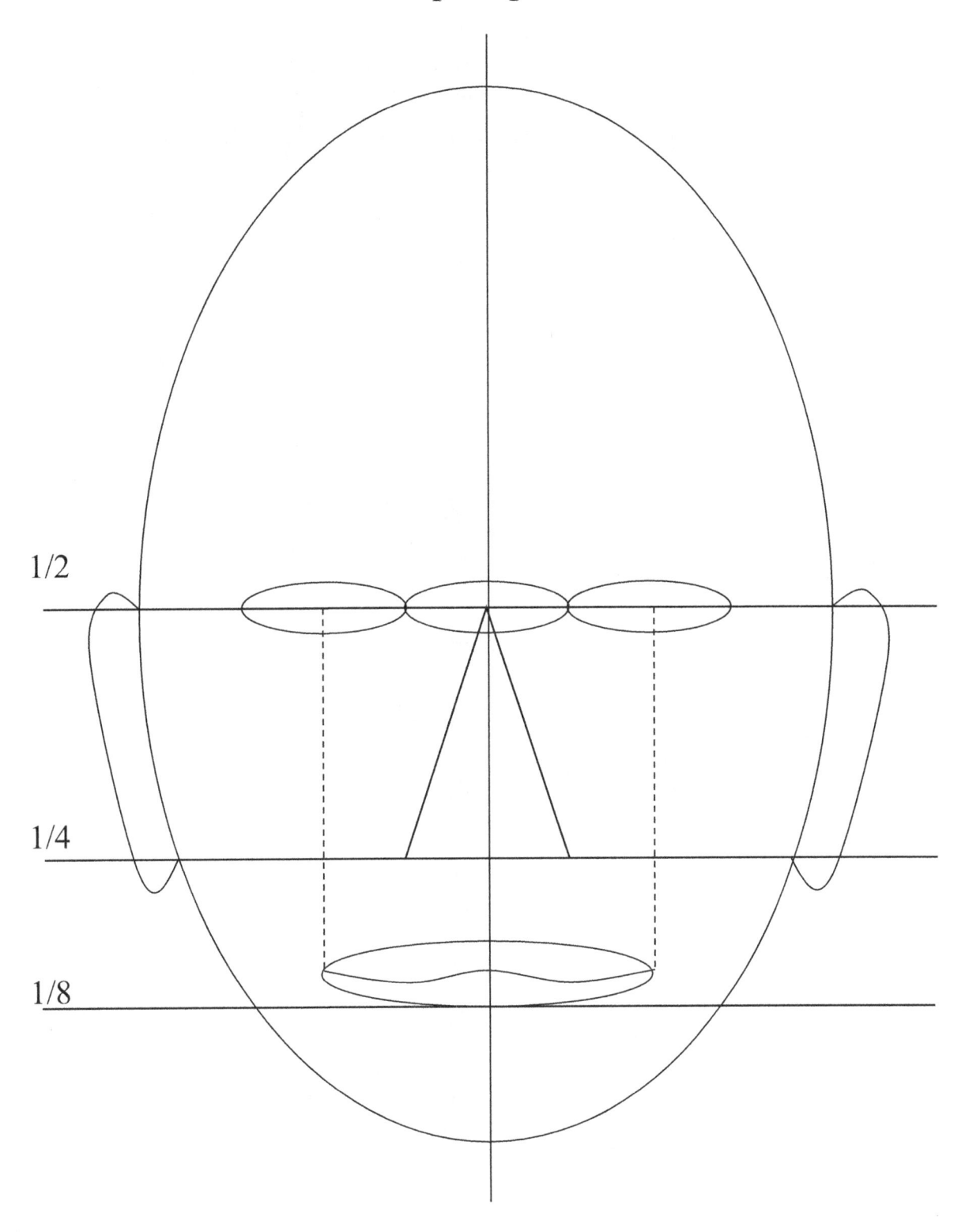

1/2

1/4

1/8

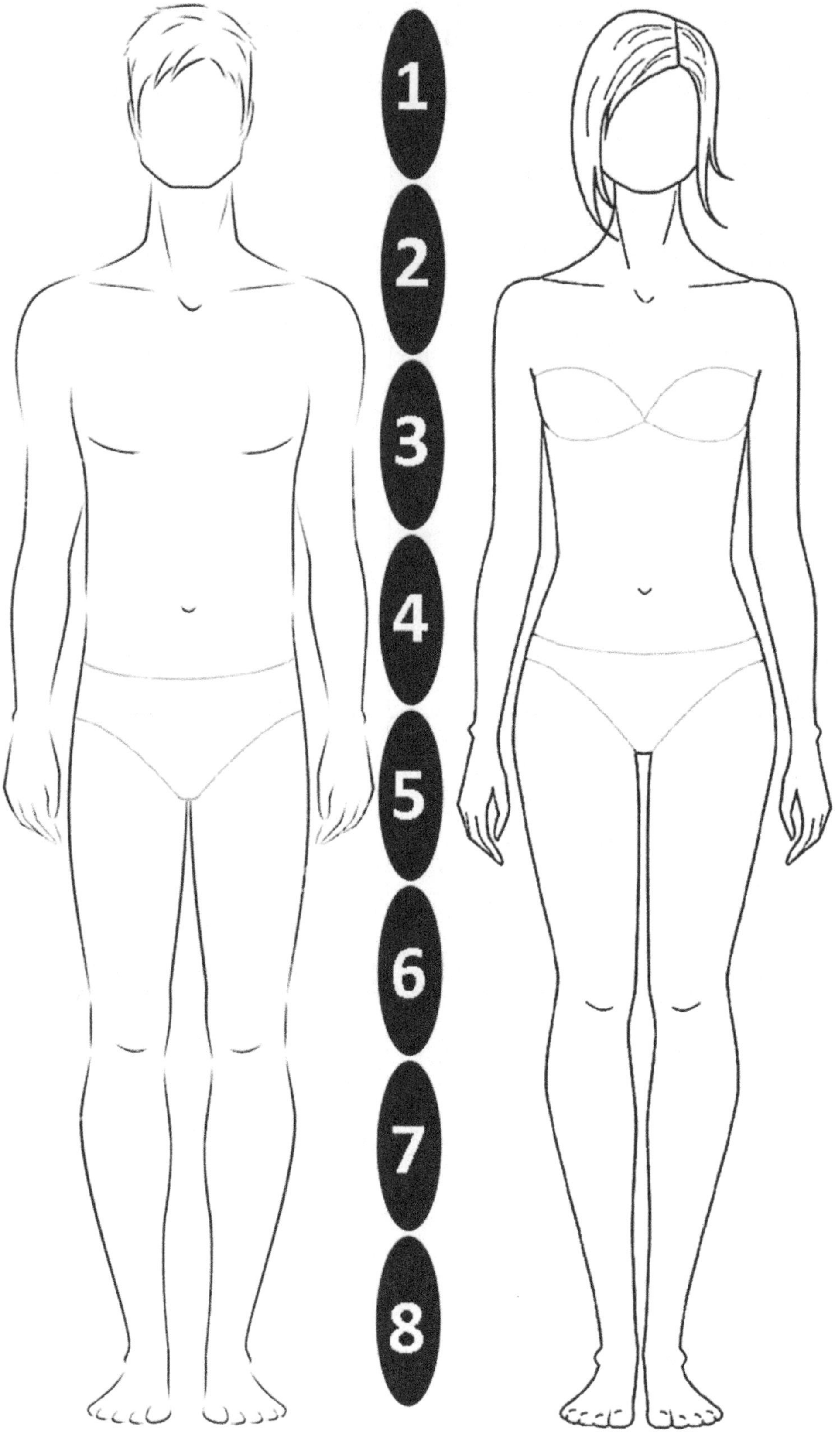
1
2
3
4
5
6
7
8

Fashion Unit:

Using these resources, you are to create 3 unique fashion designs. They must be based on human figure proportions of 8-Heads high. You may chose either male or female designs or switch them up.

You will create 3 designs:
- 1 Costume or uniform (Silly, fun, or serious)
- 1 formal (Evening gown, suit, wedding, something for a formal event)
- 1 of your personal fashion, something **YOU** might actually wear.

Before you begin, look through some magazines or other resources to find one or two items that will help inspire your 3 designs and unify them. So if you picked a Ferrari car, you might use the colors or elements for your designs, or do designs that are inspired by the ideas of speed.

Add your inspiration item(s) below:

Gesture Drawing:
To quickly catch the pose of a model in a few seconds or minutes we use gesture drawing. These are often done as a warm-up exercise for artists. Gesture drawing is not specific, but a quick general idea of the position. If done lightly, a final drawing can be worked on top of the gesture drawing. Take some times to do gesture drawings of your peers before you begin your final design. Practice making them 8-heads high.

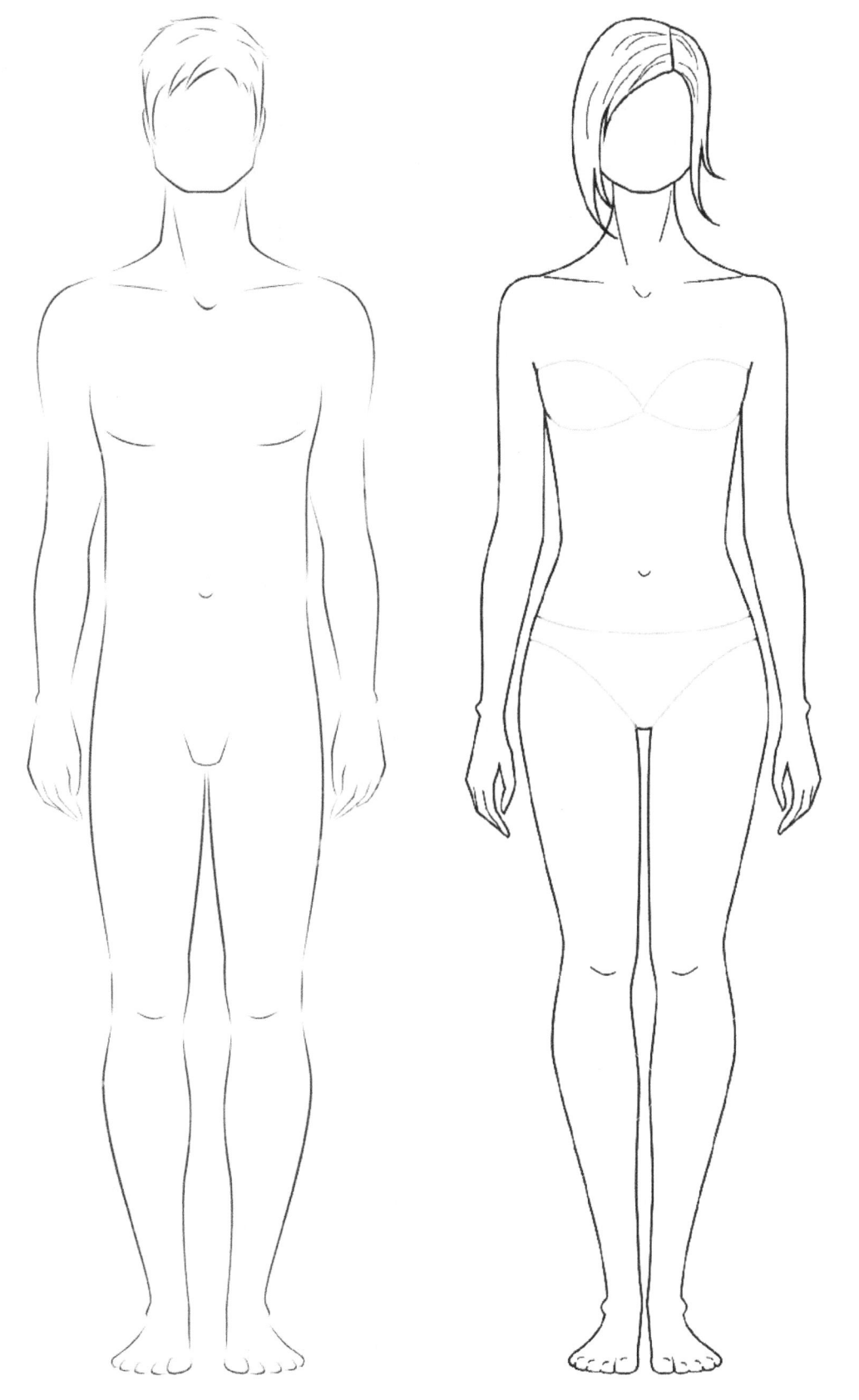

Sketch your fashion idea on top of these

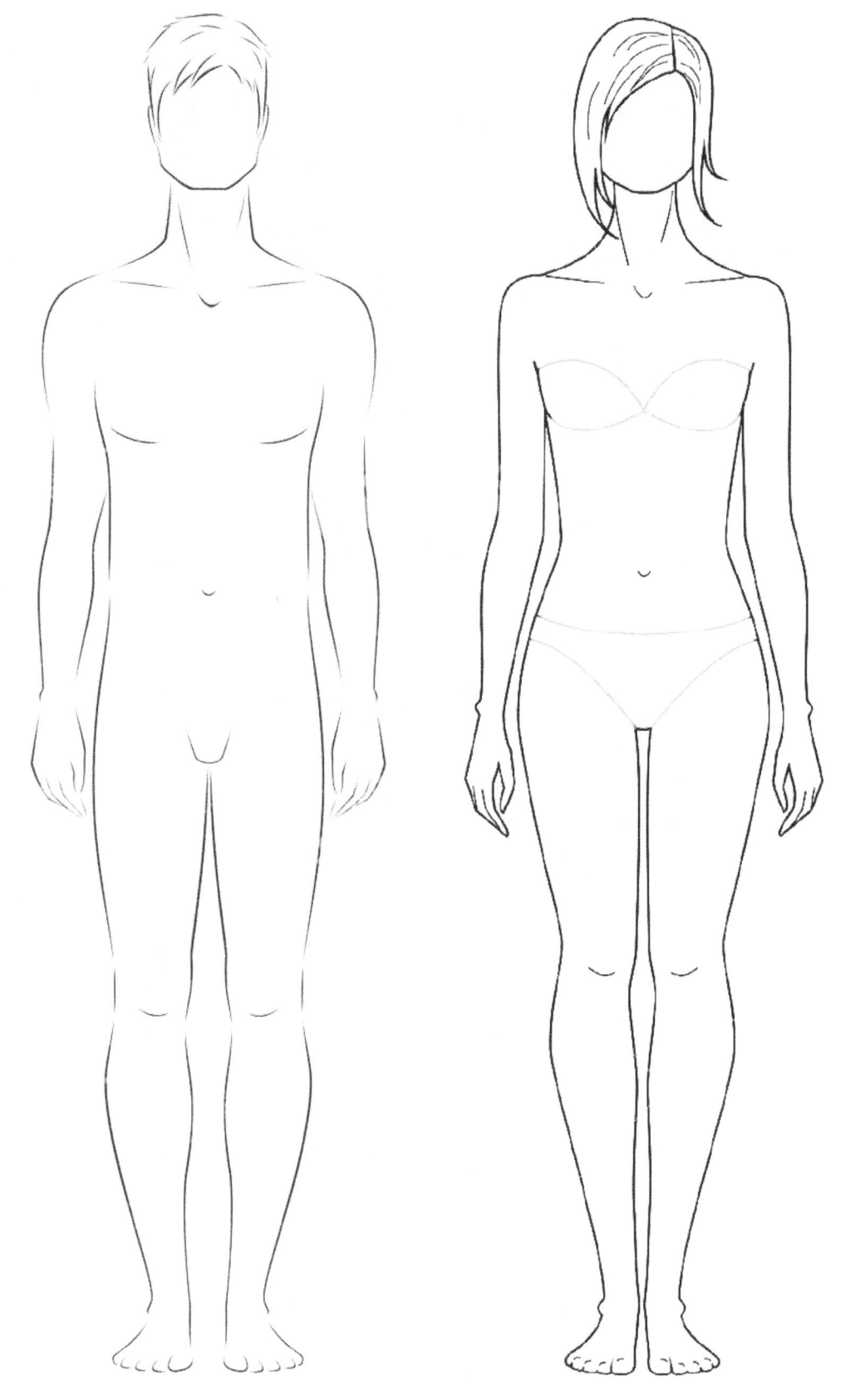

Sketch your fashion idea on top of these

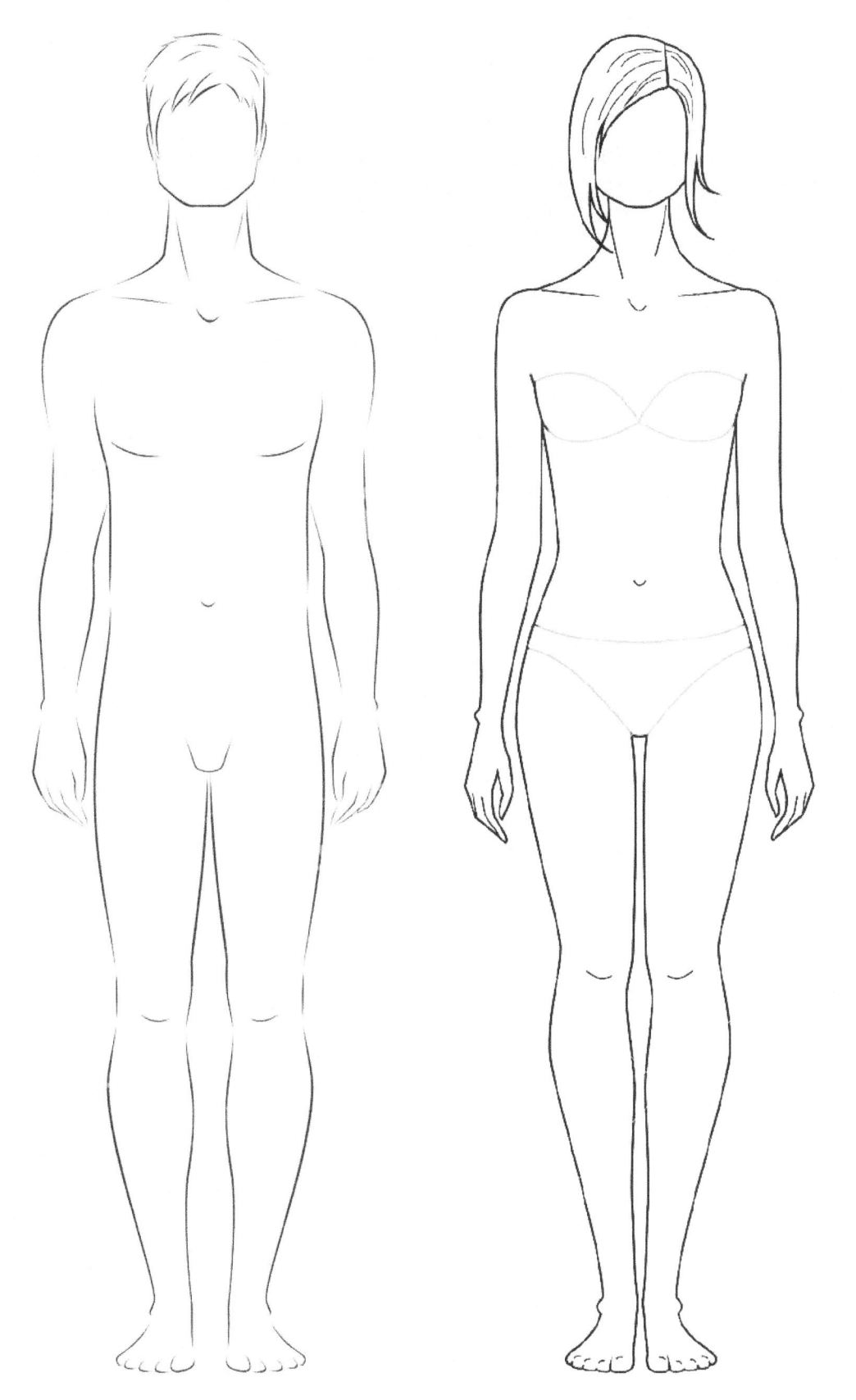

Sketch your fashion idea on top of these

Sculpture
Science Meets ART

In most cases diseases and illnesses are caused by a virus, parasite, abnormal cells, or infection. Name as many diseases or sicknesses that you can?

1.   6.

2.   7.

3.   8.

4.   9.

5.   10.

Choose one of the above illnesses. Look up what organism causes that illness, and what it looks like. Draw it below and add color too.

Your number _____ and its cause is _____

Sketch your virus project here:

Sculpting Wind

What can wind symbolize?

1. _____   2. _____

3. _____   4. _____

5. _____   6. _____

What kinds of things use wind for their form or function?

1. ___FLAGS_____   2. _____

3. _____   4. _____

5. _____   6. _____

7. _____   8. _____

9. _____   10. _____

If you had to use wind in a sculpture to show your personality, what could you create?

_____

_____

_____

_____

_____

See some examples of wind sculptures, and sketch what you might like to make below. Can you incorporate recycled materials like plastics, cans, etc?

My Cultural Background

Create a project based on information on your cultural background by creating a background pattern of repeated pattern of cultural objects and a foreground animal representing that artist's personality. Many people have different cultural backgrounds.

Cultural Background #1 (Country of origin)	Cultural Background #2 (Country of origin)	Cultural Background #3 (Country of origin)
Cultural Objects *Flowers, crafts, trees, symbols*	Cultural Objects *Flowers, crafts, trees, symbols*	Cultural Objects *Flowers, crafts, trees, symbols*
Animals from that country	Animals from that country	Animals from that country

Pick an animal and symbol for your project to represent yourself:

Create a background pattern of objects based on information above found at the library or on the internet. Then cut and paste an animal symbol for yourself on top. Any media will work for this; try colored pencil, marker, or painted paper.

Sketch Page

A Day of Dada

Dada art began about the same time as World War One (About 1916). It was a terrible war fought mostly in Europe and was thought to be the war to end all wars... but it was not. The people of Europe struggled, it was often chaotic. So awful that the Dada artists decided if the world did not make sense, their art should not make sense either! Even the name for their style was chosen by randomly placing a knife in a dictionary that happened to land on the word "Dada," a French word for 'hobbyhorse.' Marcel DuChamp was a famous Dada artist who once brought a urinal to an exhibition. He even signed it with a fake name, R. Mutt. It made people angry, they fought over it. They thought it was insulting to have a toilet in the middle of a famous gallery! Marcel laughed. You see, art is supposed to make you feel something. If the people walked into the gallery and ignored his toilet, it would have just been a toilet. But because this object, a urinal, made them angry and upset, it made them "feel" something. THEY MADE IT ART!

What are some common objects you have around you that you feel are interesting?

_____

Which one could you get and turn into a work of Dada art? _____

What is some strange or confusing name you can give it? Something in another language? Something spelled backwards? Maybe something random? You can even use your birthday to find a random name. Grab a book, and open to the page of your birth month, then count the words for your birthday. If you were born on Halloween, you would go to page 10 (October), and find the 31st word.

What name do you choose? _____

To finish your work of Dada art, you need to make a label to explain it and possibly confuse people even more. You should write a paragraph to go with your work of art. It does not have to make sense at all, but it has to sound important, and thoughtful. So if I had a paper clip, and named it "Vesuvius" this could be my paragraph:

Vesuvius was a great volcano that destroyed the civilization of Pompeii, a great and terrible tragedy that twisted the world in ways we could never imagine. This twisted piece of metal is deeply connected to the metals found under the ground and forced up to the surface by geomagnetic forces we still do not understand, like volcanoes. This junction of metal and twist is the perfect symbol of the Pompeii experience which we will never understand. As we touch paperclips on a daily basis and do not give them much thought, so too we ignore the people and city of Pompeii.

My Dada art object is _____

My title for my Dada object is: _____

_____

My explanation for my art is : _____

_____

_____

_____

_____

_____

_____

_____

_____

_____

_____

_____

Share your writing, and have a classmate make some suggestions here to improve or focus it:

_____

_____

_____

NUMBERS as a Theme

Create a painting, illustration or sculpture based on a number theme.
Work as a group or individually. Research and find more
About your chosen topic, or discover a new one!

2
Good and evil
Yin and Yang
Noah's Ark, 2 of each animal
Twins

3
Holy Trinity
Ages of man
Branches of government
Strikes
Jewels of Buddhism
Pure Ones of Taoism
Hear no evil, see no evil, speak no evil

4
Seasons
Beauties of China
Elements
Archangels in Islam
Four Horsemen of the Apocalypse
The four Gospels

5
Fingers
Books of Moses and Psalms
Basic pillars of Islam
Mayan Worlds
In India, mythological headless male warriors

6
Tastes
Foods placed on the Passover Seder Plate
Articles of belief of Islam.
Degrees of Separation
Cardinal directions: N. S. E. W, up, and down

7
Deadly sins
Virtues
Wonders of the world
Continents
Seas
Colors of the rainbow
Seven days of creation
Fires of hell and doors of Hell
Asian Lucky Gods

8
Days of Hanukkah
The number of Angels carrying the Throne of Allah
"The Immortals" Chinese demigods

9
Planets
Choirs of angels

10
The Commandments
Plagues
Lost Tribes
Branches of the tree of life
Canadian provinces

11
Soccer players
Cricket players
Football Players
Incarnations of Doctor Who
Guns in a military salute

12
Apostles
Cranial nerves
Olympians
Tribes of Israel
Days of Christmas
Months

13
Baker's Dozen
Attendees of the Last Supper
Witches in a coven
Colonies of the USA

Sketch Page

Sunset Silhouette

STEP 1: Starting from the bottom with YELLOW, create stripes of color that OVERLAP a little from one color to the next. (About 1 inch of overlap.)

STEP 2: Use the corner of a 6x folded piece of paper towel to blend the colors. be sure the transition from one color to the next is smooth and well blended.

Step 3: Add a horizon with a dark cool color, and fill in below it.

Step 4: Add a tree and 2 objects in black to your picture. Avoid putting things ON the horizon, they should be a bit below.

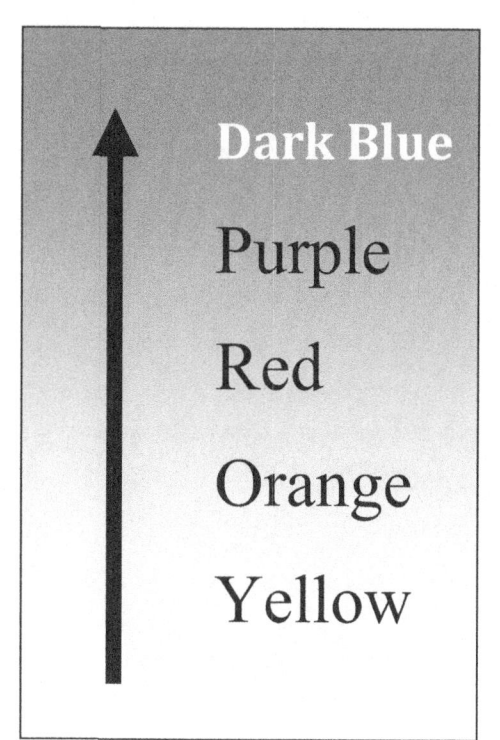

Dark Blue

Purple

Red

Orange

Yellow

Sketch Page

Comic Book Ideas
https://bit.ly/ComicLesson

Parody: Making fun of something, twisting what you know for a comic effect.

Superman → Stupidman
Terminator → Worminator
Godzilla → Tellitubbyzilla
Lord of The Rings → Lord of the Ring-Dings

What are a few movies you could make fun of?

_____ → _____

_____ → _____

_____ → _____

Try changing the title of something for a funny idea…

Teenage Mutant Ninja _____
Killer _____ from Outer Space
Attack of the Mutant _____

Your idea: _____

Try a new situation…

    Iron Man vs. Barney
    T-Rex comes to Sesame Street
    The President visits our school

Your idea: _____

There are millions of possibilities!

Do you cartoon already and have an original character???
This is a great chance to make THAT look professional.

ORIGINALITY COUNTS: Don't COPY known work.

For full credit, comic books need to include title, subtitle, dramatic action, logo, foreground, middle-ground, and background, items exiting the page, and overlap.

ME as a comic book character:

List 5 super powers you wish you had.

___: _____
___: _____
___: _____
___: _____
___: _____

Go back and number them from most to least favorite.

List 3 of your unique fashion/physical features (Glasses, headband, tattoo?)

1. _____
2. _____
3. _____

Would you be a hero or villain? _____
Why? _____
_____

What might your super name be? _____

What would be an amazing thing or adventure you could do as that character?
_____
_____

Both villains and heroes usually have side-kicks. Who/what would be your side kick?
_____

What would be their lame super power? *(It can't be as good as yours 'cause they're a side kick)*
_____
_____

On sketch paper do a sketch of how you and your sidekick might look like. Your character may look VERY different than you, but there should be some connection to them. Be sure your character also has your 3 features. If you always wear glasses, your character might also. (You can fix/change/adjust those if you like)

Title, subtitle, dramatic action, logo, foreground, middle-ground, background, items exiting the page, and overlap.

Sketch Page

Expressive Words	**Compound Words**
Love	Horseshoe
Hate	House fly
Flight	Dragonfly
Death	Football
Burial	Hotdog
Crazy	Rainbow
Strong	Waterfall
Sad	Groundhog
Depressed	Butterfly
Suicidal	Fireman
Hopeful	Firefighter
Grace	Dog food
Dirty	Toenail
Disgrace	Jellyfish
Shame	Starfish
Pride	Catfish…
Hero	Family tree
Sinful	Football…
Pius	Carpet
Travel	Honeybee
Risk	Hairnet
Anger	Hairspray
Contentment	Cheese grater
Gluttony	French fry
Lazy	French toast
Narcissism	Hummingbird
Turmoil	Pancake
Heaven	Shoehorn
Hell	Boxing ring
Regal	Earring
Eternal	
Complex	Other?
Simplicity	_____

Tutorial: https://youtu.be/sXqHFBHTlyw

Sketch Page

JABBERWOCKY
Lewis Carroll
(from *Through the Looking-Glass*, 1872)

`Twas brillig, and the slithy toves
  Did gyre and gimble in the wabe;
All mimsy were the borogoves,
  And the mome raths outgrabe.

"Beware the Jabberwock, my son!
  The jaws that bite, the claws that catch!
Beware the Jubjub bird, and shun
  The frumious Bandersnatch!"

He took his vorpal sword in hand:
  Long time the manxome foe he sought --
So rested he by the Tumtum tree,
  And stood awhile in thought.

And, as in uffish thought he stood,
  The Jabberwock, with eyes of flame,
Came whiffling through the tulgey wood,
  And burbled as it came!

One, two! One, two! And through and through
  The vorpal blade went snicker-snack!
He left it dead, and with its head
  He went galumphing back.

"And, has thou slain the Jabberwock?
  Come to my arms, my beamish boy!
O frabjous day! Callooh! Callay!"
  He chortled in his joy.

`Twas brillig, and the slithy toves
  Did gyre and gimble in the wabe;
All mimsy were the borogoves,
  And the mome raths outgrabe.

Try and do a translation of each stanza, Remember, often there is no correct answer, but there is a story here…

Repeated from above, no translation needed.

Sketch Page

This choice board can be helpful in coming up with an idea for an independent project.

Choice Board

Pick one from each column and explore.

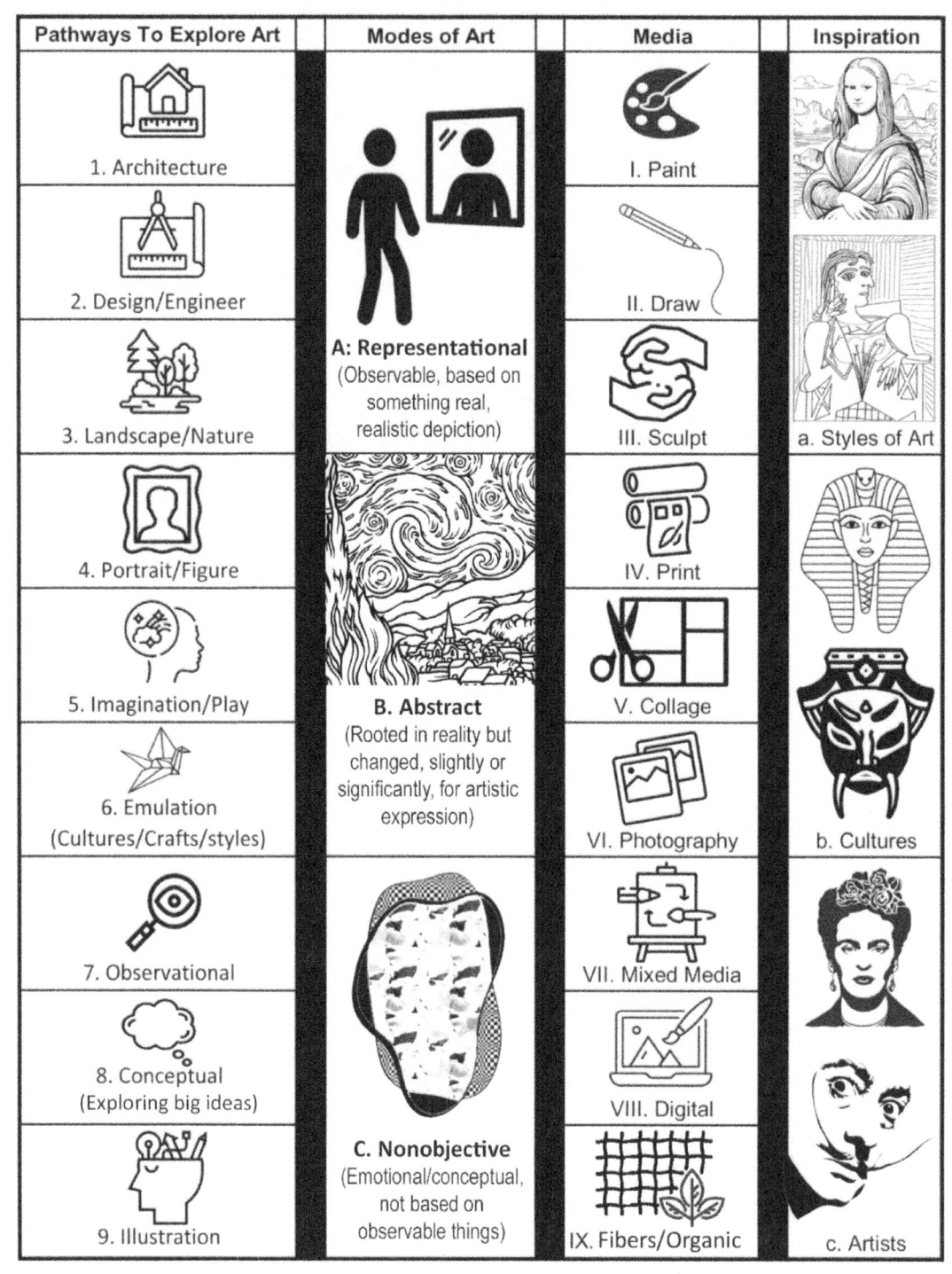

Pathways To Explore Art	Modes of Art	Media	Inspiration
1. Architecture	**A: Representational** (Observable, based on something real, realistic depiction)	I. Paint	a. Styles of Art
2. Design/Engineer		II. Draw	
3. Landscape/Nature		III. Sculpt	
4. Portrait/Figure	**B. Abstract** (Rooted in reality but changed, slightly or significantly, for artistic expression)	IV. Print	b. Cultures
5. Imagination/Play		V. Collage	
6. Emulation (Cultures/Crafts/styles)		VI. Photography	
7. Observational	**C. Nonobjective** (Emotional/conceptual, not based on observable things)	VII. Mixed Media	c. Artists
8. Conceptual (Exploring big ideas)		VIII. Digital	
9. Illustration		IX. Fibers/Organic	

Independent Project 1: Choose a School of Art, Culture, or Artist

Inspirational Topic: _____ Date(s) _____

About the topic: _____

_____

Name 4 famous examples:

1. _____ by _____ Year _____

2. _____ by _____ Year _____

3. _____ by _____ Year _____

4. _____ by _____ Year _____

What do all these works have in common?

_____

_____

_____

What specific themes, ideas, impact, or techniques came from this work?

_____

_____

_____

What could I create that might be inspired by these works, themes, ideas, or techniques?

Three Ideas:

1. _____

2. _____

3. _____

Create a sketch/thumbnail for one of these ideas.

Project Progress Document   Name _____ pd ____

This paper will document your daily participation, progress, feedback, & grade.

Project Title: _____

My reference or inspirations for this project is: _____

My personal connection: _____

_____

Intro. date   ___/___/_____

DEADLINE: ___/___/_____

Requirements:

1. _____

2. _____

3. _____

To exceed expectations, I can…

1. _____

2. _____

3. _____

Peer Feedback by _____

Actionable advice for success: _____

_____

…Instructor Section Only…

10% _____   Sketch

20% _____

25% _____ (quarter)

30 % _____   Project Work Phase

40% _____

50% _____ (half)

60% _____

70% _____

75% _____ (3/4)

80% _____   Detail & finishing

85% _____

90% _____

95% _____
(Percent complete, not a grade)

_____

_____

_____

I will take this advice: [__] Yes or [__] No thank you.

Name _____ Title _____ Pd._____

Universal Art Project Rubric

	Criteria					Points
	100% / 20pts Exceeds Expectations	90% / 18pts Meets Expectations	80% / 16pts Approaches Exp.	70% - 65% / 14pts Missed Exp.	0/F	
Project Requirements	I exceeded expectations by:	Expected use & combination of art elements & principles. Work included all requirements.	Acceptable use of art elements & principles but lacked depth in exploring requirements.	Lacks evidence of thoughtful use of elements & principles & minimally met required components.		____
Process, Research & Documentation	I exceeded expectations by:	Research & documentation are present & meet expectations. Prewriting & sketches are complete & purposeful.	Research and/or documentation is present but thin. Artist did not fully take advantage of pre-work opportunities.	Research and/or documentation was missing & had a negative impact on the final work. Evidence of depth was lacking.		____
Time & Management	I exceeded expectations by:	Student was mostly independently motivated with a few social and/or digital distractions. Work was mostly self-driven.	Student was sometimes distracted from work **OR** finished early without using the extra time to exceed expectations or stay active in art-making.	Often reminded to stay on task. Social/digital interactions impeded work. Lack of focus had a strong impact on project work.		____
Detail, Complexity, Craftsmanship, & Care	I exceeded expectations by:	Media is without folds/rips or evidence of poor handling. Materials & techniques were explored & met handling expectations. Visual challenges were attempted.	Media handling could have avoided minor rips or folds. Media or technique was not fully explored. Visual challenges were minimal.	Poor handling or storage had an impact. Media & techniques show little evidence of exploration. Visual challenges were avoided.		____
Original, Personal, & Unique (Always credit your inspirations)	100% original & highly personal because:	Generally personal & unique but inspired by:	Topically personalized & based on:	Topical & highly derivative of:	Copied	
Comments:					**Grade** ____	

Created by www.artedguru.com & www.FirehousePublications.com

If you could do this project again, what might you do differently?

This choice board can be helpful in coming up with an idea for an independent project.

Choice Board

Pick one from each column and explore.

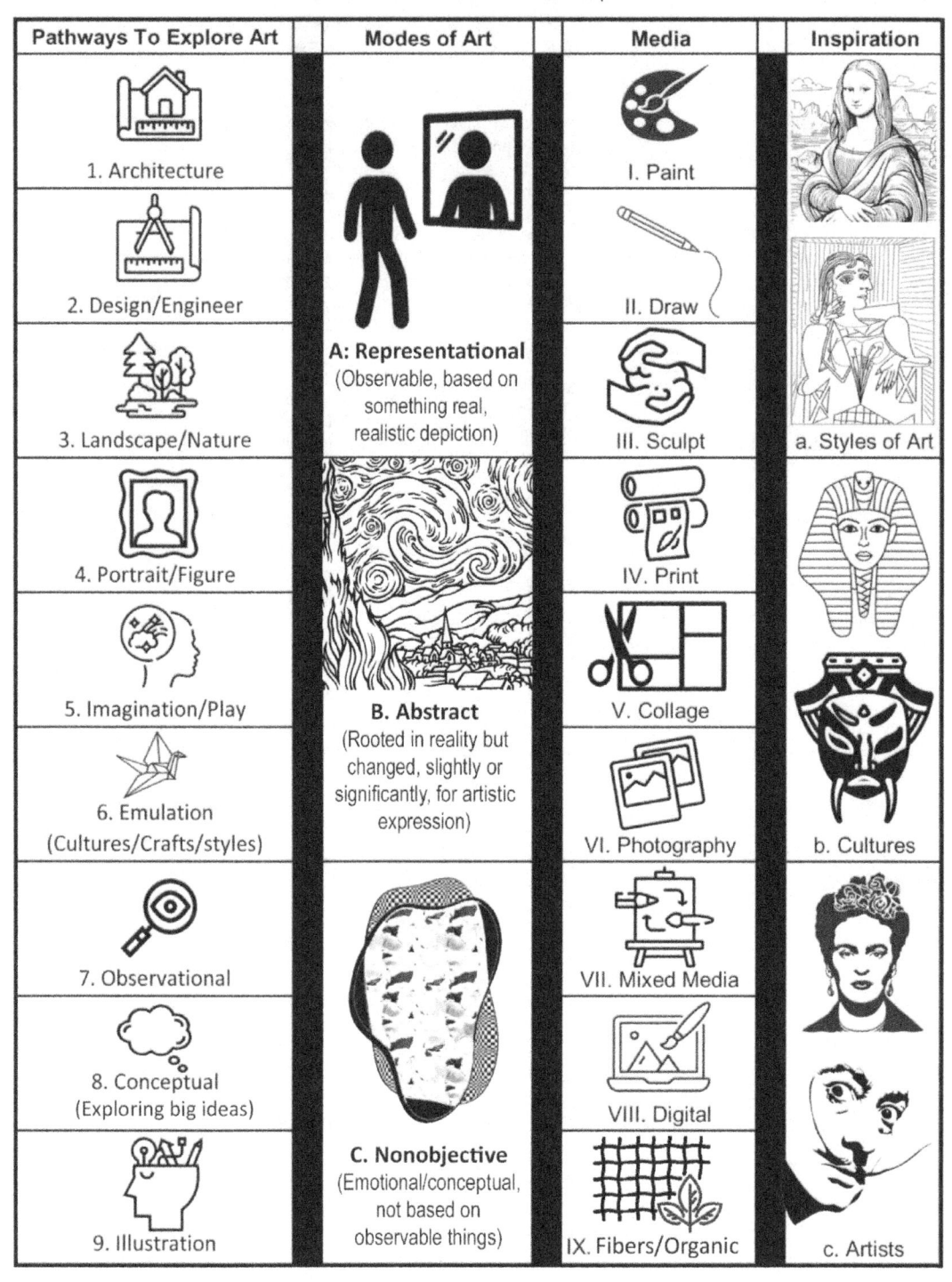

Pathways To Explore Art	Modes of Art	Media	Inspiration
1. Architecture	**A: Representational** (Observable, based on something real, realistic depiction)	I. Paint	a. Styles of Art
2. Design/Engineer		II. Draw	
3. Landscape/Nature		III. Sculpt	
4. Portrait/Figure	**B. Abstract** (Rooted in reality but changed, slightly or significantly, for artistic expression)	IV. Print	b. Cultures
5. Imagination/Play		V. Collage	
6. Emulation (Cultures/Crafts/styles)		VI. Photography	
7. Observational	**C. Nonobjective** (Emotional/conceptual, not based on observable things)	VII. Mixed Media	c. Artists
8. Conceptual (Exploring big ideas)		VIII. Digital	
9. Illustration		IX. Fibers/Organic	

Independent Project 2: Choose a School of Art, Culture, or Artist

Inspirational Topic: _____ Date(s) _____

About the topic: _____
_____

Name 4 famous examples:

1. _____ by _____ Year _____

2. _____ by _____ Year _____

3. _____ by _____ Year _____

4. _____ by _____ Year _____

What do all these works have in common?

_____

_____

_____

What specific themes, ideas, impact, or techniques came from this work?

_____

_____

_____

What could I create that might be inspired by these works, themes, ideas, or techniques?

Three Ideas:

1. _____

2. _____

3. _____

Create a sketch/thumbnail for one of these ideas.

Project Progress Document   Name _____ pd ____

This paper will document your daily participation, progress, feedback, & grade.

Project Title: _____

My reference or inspirations for this project is: _____

My personal connection: _____

_____

Intro. date   ___/___/_____

DEADLINE: ___/___/_____

Requirements:

1. _____

2. _____

3. _____

To exceed expectations, I can…

1. _____

2. _____

3. _____

Peer Feedback by _____

Actionable advice for success: _____

_____

_____

…Instructor Section Only…

10% _____   ⎫ Sketch

20% _____

25% _____ (quarter)

30 % _____   ⎫ Project Work Phase

40% _____

50% _____ (half)

60% _____

70% _____

75% _____ (3/4)

80% _____   ⎫ Detail & finishing

85% _____

90% _____

95% _____

(Percent complete, not a grade)

_____

_____

I will take this advice: [__] Yes or [__] No thank you.

Name _____ Title _____ Pd._____

Universal Art Project Rubric

	Criteria				Points
	100% / 20pts Exceeds Expectations	90% / 18pts Meets Expectations	80% / 16pts Approaches Exp.	70% - 65% / 14pts Missed Exp.	0/F
Project Requirements	I exceeded expectations by:	Expected use & combination of art elements & principles. Work included all requirements.	Acceptable use of art elements & principles but lacked depth in exploring requirements.	Lacks evidence of thoughtful use of elements & principles & minimally met required components.	____
Process, Research & Documentation	I exceeded expectations by:	Research & documentation are present & meet expectations. Prewriting & sketches are complete & purposeful.	Research and/or documentation is present but thin. Artist did not fully take advantage of pre-work opportunities.	Research and/or documentation was missing & had a negative impact on the final work. Evidence of depth was lacking.	____
Time & Management	I exceeded expectations by:	Student was mostly independently motivated with a few social and/or digital distractions. Work was mostly self-driven.	Student was sometimes distracted from work **OR** finished early without using the extra time to exceed expectations or stay active in art-making.	Often reminded to stay on task. Social/digital interactions impeded work. Lack of focus had a strong impact on project work.	____
Detail, Complexity, Craftsmanship, & Care	I exceeded expectations by:	Media is without folds/rips or evidence of poor handling. Materials & techniques were explored & met handling expectations. Visual challenges were attempted.	Media handling could have avoided minor rips or folds. Media or technique was not fully explored. Visual challenges were minimal.	Poor handling or storage had an impact. Media & techniques show little evidence of exploration. Visual challenges were avoided.	____
Original, Personal, & Unique (Always credit your inspirations)	100% original & highly personal because:	Generally personal & unique but inspired by:	Topically personalized & based on:	Topical & highly derivative of:	Copied

Comments:

Grade ____

Created by www.artedguru.com & www.FirehousePublications.com

If you could do this project again, what might you do differently?

Art Quotes: Short Writing

A: Please take 2 or 3 minutes to write about the following quote.

What is meant by the following quote?

"Painting is easy when you don't know how, but very difficult when you do."

~ Edgar Degas   Video: http://y2u.be/W5PrQiJVWW8

_____

_____

_____

B: Please take 2 or 3 minutes to write about the following quote.

What is meant by the following quote?

Your ego can become an obstacle to your work. If you start believing in your greatness, it is the death of your creativity. ~ Marina Abramovic   Video: http://y2u.be/IhbiVceuR0o

_____

_____

_____

C: Please take 2 or 3 minutes to write about the following quote.

What is meant by the following quote?

In speaking of his time as a child in a mental institution, "They took the clay away – child abuse" ~Alonzo Clemons, *"Savant, Sculptor and Artist" 05/10/19*   http://y2u.be/RrW4upZoXHA

_____

_____

_____

D: Please take 2 or 3 minutes to write about the following quote.

What is meant by the following quote?

"I make my art in silence. The materials conjure ideas. The ideas conjure images. The images conjure art. The art conjures feelings. The feelings are the goal." ~Betye Saar

Video: http://y2u.be/T7CFz9xzhIM

_____

_____

_____

E: Please take 2 or 3 minutes to write about the following quote.

What is meant by the following quote?

"I realized at a young age that art was there for me to create conversation and a relationship with people. It allowed me to become approachable to my peers, who might not have otherwise understood me." ~ Alana Tillman Video: http://y2u.be/W0FEY6JWdUE

_____

_____

_____

F: Please take 2 or 3 minutes to write about the following quote.

What is meant by the following quote?

Art builds empathy and an understanding of other humans that will lead us to see ourselves in one another, and thus grow a family rather than a society. This is about how beautiful we are when we get to see all of us. ~ Roberto Lugo   Video http://y2u.be/NH02Hrj60B0

_____

_____

_____

G: Please take 2 or 3 minutes to write about the following quote.

What is meant by the following quote?

For me, art can reflect the celebration of the simple and good things in life. This is most important to me! ~Romero Britto Video: http://y2u.be/nZFIHI0MOnY

_____

_____

_____

H: Please take 2 or 3 minutes to write about the following quote.

What is meant by the following quote?

"Every idea occurs while you are working. If you are sitting around waiting for inspiration, you could sit there forever." ~ Chuck Close Video: http://y2u.be/tXsuo4NWOUY

_____

_____

_____

I: Please take 2 or 3 minutes to write about the following quote.

What is meant by the following quote?

"A true artist is not one who is inspired, but one who inspires others. What is important is to spread confusion, not eliminate it." ~Salvador Dali'

Video: https://vimeo.com/145418153

_____

_____

_____

J: Please take 2 or 3 minutes to write about the following quote.

What is meant by the following quote?

"We don't make mistakes. We just have happy accidents." ~Bob Ross

                                                                                          Video: http://y2u.be/OX-kO2eomoI

_____
_____
_____

K: Please take 2 or 3 minutes to write about the following quote.

What is meant by the following quote?

In reflecting on spending 45 year in prison for a crime he didn't commit: "I didn't actually think I'd ever be free again. This art is what I did to stay sane," ~Richard Phillips

                                                                                          Video: http://y2u.be/aWKZ9P1N-n0

_____
_____
_____

L: Please take 2 or 3 minutes to write about the following quote.

What is meant by the following quote?

"There are many accidents that are nothing but accidents-and forget it. But there are some that were brought about only because you are the person you are... you have the wherewithal, intelligence, and energy to recognize it and do something with it."

~Helen Frankenthaler   **Video: http://y2u.be/7efK8UTjlzY**

_____
_____
_____

M: Please take 2 or 3 minutes to write about the following quote.

What is meant by the following quote?

"Red is one of the strongest colors, it's blood, it has a power with the eye. That's why traffic lights are red I guess, and stop signs as well... In fact I use red in all of my paintings."
~Keith Haring   Video: http://y2u.be/8eE4Dm8EGTg

_____

_____

_____

N: Please take 2 or 3 minutes to write about the following quote.

What is meant by the following quote?

What's important about the artists we learn about in art history and see in all the art books is that they have somehow pushed the boundaries of what people think art is or should be, and that's how they've made their work relevant. That's what I'm trying to figure out for myself. ~Kadir Nelson   Video: http://y2u.be/01yRoSrhQME

_____

_____

_____

O: Please take 2 or 3 minutes to write about the following quote.

What is meant by the following quote?

"Art should comfort the disturbed and disturb the comfortable." ~ Banksy

Video: http://y2u.be/MMoVoWXBorg

_____

_____

_____

P: Please take 2 or 3 minutes to write about the following quote.

After watching this video, what is meant by the following quote? http://y2u.be/cZ-j4UbyKCU

"My paintings represent my happy personality. I always want to do beautiful paintings."
~Ellen Kane

_____
_____
_____

Q: Please take 2 or 3 minutes to write about the following quote.

What is meant by the following quote?

"The idea is to make visible those who are practically invisible in the city, humanize public spaces." - VHILS (Alexandre Farto)   Video: http://y2u.be/P8_nZTVaaNw

_____
_____
_____

R: Please take 2 or 3 minutes to write about the following quote.

What is meant by the following quote?

"All of depiction is fiction, it's only a question of degree." ~Titus Kaphar

Video: http://y2u.be/_GmoWXl1uOA

_____
_____
_____

S: Please take 2 or 3 minutes to write about the following quote.

What is meant by the following quote?

"What I am seeking is not the real and not the unreal but rather the unconscious, the mystery of the instinctive in the human race." ~Amedeo Modigliani

Video: http://y2u.be/8541kuU0I8M

_____
_____
_____

T: Please take 2 or 3 minutes to write about the following quote.

What is meant by the following quote?

"If you look at the paintings that I love in art history, these are the paintings where great, powerful men are being celebrated on the big walls of museums throughout the world. What feels really strange is not to be able to see a reflection of myself in that world."
~Kehinde Wiley   Video: http://y2u.be/Q71UkyrbbRE

_____
_____
_____

U: Please take 2 or 3 minutes to write about the following quote.

What is meant by the following quote?

"I put the viewer to work, to keep them imagining." ~Shirley Woodson

Video: http://y2u.be/bKb4edvsxss

_____
_____
_____

V: Please take 2 or 3 minutes to write about the following quote.

What is meant by the following quote?

"I honestly believed everybody in the world wanted to make abstract paintings, and people only became lawyers and doctors and brokers and things because they couldn't make abstract paintings." ~Frank Stella   Video: http://y2u.be/G3rxnr8tUYA

_____

_____

_____

W: Please take 2 or 3 minutes to write about the following quote.

What is meant by the following quote?

"I'm a musician trapped in the body of a glass artist" ~Preston Singletary

Video: http://y2u.be/URItBWc5zXQ

_____

_____

_____

X: Please take 2 or 3 minutes to write about the following quote.

What is meant by the following quote?

"I don't think you can create art out of anger; it has to come out of some form of understanding. You have to feel good about who you are and that you could do something to change things." ~Faith Ringgold   Video: http://y2u.be/IZ-VvOep2D8

_____

_____

_____

Y: Please take 2 or 3 minutes to write about the following quote.

What is meant by the following quote?

"To be an artist at twenty is to be twenty: to still be an artist at fifty is to be an artist."

~E. Gibbons as inspired by Eugene Delacroix's quote about poets.

Video: http://y2u.be/V0TdVj2kCoU

___

___

___

Z: Please take 2 or 3 minutes to write about the following quote.

What is meant by the following quote?

"Painting is like a sort of sickness, I think." ~Joan Mitchell

Video: http://y2u.be/XQ0pbQf1Nqo

___

___

___

1: Write your own quote about art.

___

___

___

___

Art Principles of Design Sample

"Day and Night" by M.C. Escher

UNITY: Same-ness throughout an image:
   The whole image is in black and white unifying the picture through limited color.

VARIETY: (Contrast): Differences throughout an image
   The images have a variety of different things like birds, towns, rivers, and fields.

EMPHASIS: How one thing stands out above all others in some way.
   The white bird to the right stands out because it is so bright against the dark background.

MOVEMENT: Might be real or suggested movement..
   The birds appear to be flying in opposite directions, giving a sense of movement.

BALANCE: (Symmetrical vs Asymmetrical Balance, Predictable or non-predictable balance)
   The image above is symmetrically balanced because the left is a mirror image of the right.
   Even distribution of "visual weight."

PATTERN: (Shapes, forms, lines…) Repeated motifs that create a predictable or unpredictable pattern.
   The birds create an alternating regular pattern in both their positive and negative space.
   OR: The fields in the background make a regular pattern like a quilt.

CONTRAST: Opposites. They can be visual or suggested by mood or subject too.
   The white birds on the right are in contrast to the blue birds on the left.
   OR: The birds in the foreground appear much larger than the buildings in the background.

Emotional Values of Shapes and Colors

There are some symbols in cultures that are the same everywhere. For instance, a puddle of red will be assumed to be blood; this would be the same in New York, China, or the jungles of some far off land.

Artists have been using these cultural symbols in their art to hide the meanings of their work or to code them. Here is a simple list. Remember shapes and colors can be combined for mixed emotional values. A heart shape is a combination of circles and a triangle.

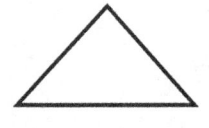

Triangles are associated with *SHARP* objects like a knife, a sword, broken glass, and spear. They are considered aggressive, dangerous, negative, and unbalanced. Triangles can be drawn in many ways to make them look more or less sharp.

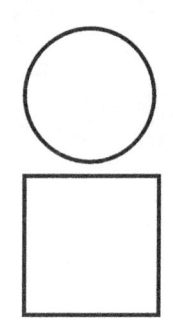

Circles are associated with SOFT objects like a balloon, bubble, or ball. They are considered playful, soft, energetic, positive, and happy.

Squares are associated with constructive ideas like building. They are regular, stable, strong, dependable, and at times, monotonous. Stretching the square into a rectangle can break up the monotony.

Red: Associated with blood, aggression, anger

Orange: Aggressive but not deadly. (Like Tackle Football)

Gold: A color of richness and wealth. Also a color of accomplishment. (Like a Gold Award)

Yellow: Playful, warm, enthusiastic, giddy, and child-like

Green: A color of growth. The type of green can indicate freshness

Blue: Associated with the sky or water, it is vast, cool, quenching, life-giving, and generally positive

Purple: A deep dark sky, royalty, peaceful, calm, and quiet

Black: A color of mystery or the unknown, also a color of heaviness and matter

Brown: Earth, soil, dirt. A color of potential growth, possibilities, a new beginning, or the end

White: A color of light, spirituality, and purity

MIXING colors will give new meanings and associations, so will using colored patterns.

Color Vocabulary

This vocabulary may be on an exam, along with your 8 Art Element Information and Art Principles of Design.

Value The intensity of a color, its saturation as compared to another color. "Pink has a lighter value than red, but a darker value than white."

Shading Changing the value by adding black or white.

Chiaroscuro Italian word for light and dark. It is the change in the highlights and shadows.

Spectrum White light separated into its primary and secondary colors. They are in order: red, orange, yellow, green, blue and purple.

Hue Is the actual color without shade or highlight.

Primary Colors The 3 colors that mix to make every other color. (red, blue, yellow)

Secondary Colors The first mixes of the primary colors. (orange, green, purple) KNOW how to make each secondary color!!!

Intermediate Colors These are the colors between the primary and secondary colors, sometimes called tertiary (Ter-She-Airy) colors.

Complementary Colors Colors on the opposite sides of the color wheel, considered direct opposites like red and green.

Analogous Colors Neighboring colors on the color wheel, like yellow and orange, or blue and green.

Monochromatic Colors Different values of the same hue or color. Changing one color from light to dark. A black and white photo is monochromatic or one all in blues…

Intensity The brightness or dullness of a color.

Color Harmonies Colors that are grouped together for effect. Generally analogous colors are considered harmonious or varying versions of a single color. (see monochromatic).

Warm Colors Colors that are more energetic and seem to come forward. When you think of fire, you'll know these colors are red, yellow and orange.

Cool Colors Colors that are less energetic and seem to recede. When you think of water, you may recall that these colors are blue, green and purple.

Sample Test

1
2
3
4
balance
black
brown
circle
color
cone
cool
cube
cylinder
dark
depth
element
form
length
light
line
mass
negative
neutral
point
positive
primary
rectangle
reflected
secondary
shadow
shape
space
sphere
square
texture
triangle
warm
white
width

All possible answers are in the list on the left. Some answers are repeated, some are never used. Crossing off answers may not be helpful. The "#" sign means the answer is a number.

A line is a _____ moving through _____. We can measure the _____ of a line and nothing else, therefore it is _#_____ dimensional or _#_____ -D.

A _____ that intersects itself will create a shape. A shape is _#_____ dimensional. There are _#_____ basic shapes. The one with the fewest amount of sides is the _____, and the one with the most sides is the _____.

A _____ that moves in _____ can create a form. There are _#_____ basic forms. The one with the fewest amount of sides is the _____. The one with the most sides is the _____.

There are _#_____ basic colors. Basic colors are also called _____ colors. When these basic colors mix they create _____ colors of which there are _#_____. Color is _____ light. Orange, Red and Yellow are considered _____ colors, while Blue, Green and Purple are considered _____ colors.

_____ refers to the weight of something; sometimes it is real and sometimes it is the way it looks. A _____ colored box will look heavier than a _____ colored one.

The roughness or smoothness of a surface refers to its _____. It can sometimes be made by repeating an art _____ many times.

All objects, art and non-art, take up _____. Many art elements move through it. This art element comes in 2 types, they are _____ meaning where the object IS, and _____, meaning where the object is NOT.

The art element of _____ helps us see all other art elements. We see everything because it is _____ off of an object or surface and back to our eye. When it is NOT bounced back to us we see _____.

120

8 Art Elements Review

USE this information **WITH** Art Principles! Principles **organize** the Elements!

A **line** is a point moving through space. We can measure the length of a line and nothing else about it; therefore it is one-dimensional or 1-D.

A line that intersects itself will create a **shape**. A shape is 2-dimensional. There are 3 basic shapes. They are the triangle, circle, and square.

A shape that moves in space can create a **form**. There are 4 basic forms. They are the cylinder, cone, cube, and sphere.

There are 3 basic **colors**. Basic colors are also called primary colors. When these basic colors mix they create secondary colors of which there are 3. Color is reflected light. Orange, red, and yellow are considered warm colors, while blue, green, and purple are considered cool colors. KNOW color wheel and mixtures!!!! Complementary = opposite, analogous = neighboring.

Mass refers to the weight of something, sometimes it is real and sometimes it is the way it looks. A dark colored box will look heavier than a light colored one.*

The roughness or smoothness of a surface refers to its **texture**. It can sometimes be made by repeating an art element many times. For example if you draw 100 lines, they will no longer be seen as lines, but as a texture; like grass.

All objects, art and non-art, take up **space**. Many art elements move through it. This art element comes in 2 types; Positive Space, meaning where the object IS, and Negative Space, meaning where the object is NOT.

The art element of **light** helps us see all other art elements. We see everything because it is reflected off an object or surface and back to our eyes. When it is NOT bounced back to us, we see black, or nothing.*

***Mass** and **Light** are sometimes combined and called **VALUE**. When discussing 3D art Mass and light are important to separate, while 2D art often combines these elements. It is how artists create the illusion of an object looking like it is 3D when really it is on a flat surface. It is done through shading and highlighting with many techniques.

Principles of Design

What does **Balance** Mean? Having an equal amount of stuff or visual weight in an artwork.

Symmetrical Balance = Perfect Balance.

Asymmetrical Balance = Unequal stuff, but still in balance, (A brick /giant bag of feathers)

What does **Movement** Mean? Having a sense of direction, sometimes actual movement (like in a mobile) In a cartoon it can be shown with "swish lines", in a painting it may be in a blur, or an area where there is gradual or rapid change or repetition. Blur in a photograph indicates movement.

Does a sculpture have to actually move to have "Movement?" NO, it only needs to look like it could move.

What is **Rhythm**? Repeated elements making a visual rhythm.

It organizes space through repetition. This repetition can be predictable, complicated or unpredictable.

Does it have to be regular (predictable)? No, When unpredictable, we call that "organic" or of nature.

What is **Variety**? Having a diverse mixture of any art element, like shape or color to avoid monotony or boredom in a work of art. A painting that includes many colors, not just one or two.

What is **Contrast**? Juxtaposition. To put opposites in the same image to make each stand out. Opposites colors like red and green, or opposite shapes like circular and sharp shapes, areas of light and dark.

What is the opposite of contrast? Unity or harmony. Remember that any art element can be contrasted, just find its opposite. There are 8 art elements like line, shape, color, form, light, texture, mass, and space.

What is **Emphasis**? A highlight of a particular area or thing.

Should the focal point be centered in an artwork? Not usually, but it can. A *little* off center is often true.

Where should it go? Anywhere but the center. As a general rule, putting something in the center of a painting makes it feel less like movement, like a portrait. Moving it to the side, a bit, makes it seem that it has a bit more visual energy.

What is **Pattern**? A repeated art element can create a pattern, like a repeated shape on a quilt, fabric, even leaves on a tree can be a pattern, though we would call that an organic (unpredictable) pattern.

What kind of artists use pattern? (Architects: brick pattern in a wall. Quilter...)

What 2 kinds of pattern are possible? Predictable (mechanical) and unpredictable (organic).

What is **Unity**? Having similarity in some way through an art element or material or theme. Like everything being red, or all parts made from squares...

What is the opposite of Unity? Contrast.

Please Note: Color mixtures, complimentary colors, analogous colors, triads, what colors mix well, which ones do not, primary colors, and secondary colors.

Schools of Art - History

A "School Of Art" is another way to say a group of art or a style of art. We put things in groups all the time. We can put people in groups too like girls and boys. Religions are kinds of groups like Christians, Muslims, Jews, and Buddhists… Even your pets are put in groups like poodles, bull dogs, spaniels, and beagles…

We group these things by the way they look. Poodles all have curly hair, Dalmatians have black spots, Beagles are smaller and have brown spots.

Art is the same way. If you see a painting, with people wearing rich clothes like from a Cinderella Movie, and the trees look very fluffy, and the people look like they are rich and playing around, then it might be from the Rococo (Row-co-co) school of art.

If you see a painting of something you might see in a TV commercial, and it has very bright colors, it might be from the Pop Art school of art.

Rococo and Pop Art are schools of art. We will learn about 13 important ones. You should know there are hundreds of schools of art, but you will learn about just a few important ones. They are:

Renaissance (Re-na-sance)
Baroque (Ba-roke)
Rococo (Row-co-co)
Neo-Classical (Neo-Clas-si-kul)
Romanticism (Ro-man-ti-si-zum)
Realism (real-is-um)
Impressionism (Imm-pre-shon-is-um)
Cubism (Qb-is-um) or (Cube-is-um)
Dada (Da-da)
Surrealism (Sur-real-is-um)
Expressionism (X-pre-shun-is-um)
Abstract Expressionism (Ab-stract, X-pre-shun-is-um)
Pop Art

Tutorials: https://bit.ly/SchoolsOfArt

Research:

Pick one school of art from the previous page. Maybe your teacher will have you pick from a hat, so not everyone does the same thing. Write it here:

_____

Use the internet or the library to answer these questions:

1. What is the year that your school of art began? _____*
(* this may not be exact, but get as close as you can)

2. Name three artists of your school of art and their birth year

_____ born in _____

_____ born in _____

_____ born in _____

3. Many artists start after they are 20 years old. If you add 20 to their birth year, is your answer to number 1 still correct? Do you need to change it?

4. Name three famous artworks (painting, drawing, or sculpture) and the artist.

_____ made by _____

_____ made by _____

_____ made by _____

5. What must art from your school of art need to look like to be from that style?

_____

_____

_____

_____

POSTERS:

Working with a small group of two to four people, you are to create a poster that will teach others about that school of art.

Who is in your group? (Put your name in too)

_____,

_____,

_____,

_____,

RULES: You must include:
- Title (That's the school of art)
- General dates of the school of art
- ART from that period IN COLOR (You may photocopy and color in)
- Label all artwork

Written information should include:
- Written history of that school of art
- 4 or more artists working in that period
- Each artist must be shown with an artwork on the poster
- CLUES: If you saw a painting, how would you know it was from your "School Of Art" List some clues to know how to know the art's school

Do a bit more like…
- Include an interesting fact like –Van Gogh went crazy because he held his brushes in his mouth and got slowly poisoned by his paint!
- QUOTE: Include a famous quote from artist in your school of art.

There is a sample poster on the next page and a sketch page after that.

Schools of Art Poster Project Sample by Students

Poster planning sketch page. School of art: _____

Interview

With a Dead Artist!

Cover Art by Douglas A. Sirois

Some Dead Artists

This is not to be considered a complete list of possible artists.

Pablo Picasso
Marcel Duchamp
Henri Matisse
Vincent Van Gogh
Claude Monet
Édouard Manet
Georgia O'Keeffe
Piet Mondrian
Paul Klee
Roy Lichtenstein
Elizabeth Catlett
Michelangelo
Salvador Dali
Jackson Pollack
Edmonia Lewis
Mark Rothko
Paul Cezanne
Andy Warhol
Ansel Adams
Georges Seurat
Robert Rauschenberg
Albers Joseph
Albrecht Dürer
Paul Gauguin
Louise Bourgeois
Francisco Goya
Jean-Michel Basquiat
Robert Indiana
Berthe Morisot
Joan Miró
Gustave Courbet

Grant Wood
Andrew Wyeth
Pierre Renoir
M. C. Escher
Mary Cassatt
Alexander Calder
Rembrandt Van Rijn
George Rodrigue
Dorothea Lang
Edvard Munch
Laura Knight
Duane Hanson
Louise Nevelson
Agnes Martin
Frida Kahlo
Katsushika Hokusai
Edward Hopper
Jacob Lawrence
Rosa Bonheur
Henri Rousseau
Marc Chagall
Augustus Rodin
Tamara de Lempicka
Norman Rockwell
George Segal
Grandma Moses
Elaine de Kooning
Willem de Kooning
Jacques-Louis David
Bob Ross
Dorothea Tanning

The Scenario!

The dead have come to life again! You'd think the government would be on high alert, schools would be closed, and there would be chaos everywhere... but no. Unlike pop-culture zombie movies, these dead folks are just as normal as they ever were. Most zombies have happily found jobs at McDonald's and Walmart.

Your art teacher, apparently a zombie sympathizer, has decided that this is the perfect opportunity for you to actually go out and meet a famous artist and interview them instead of writing a boring research paper.

The next few pages offer you 50 potential questions to ask, ***TOO MANY***, but your goal is to ask enough to fill out _____ full pages of interview. You can always do more but don't do less.

Other Artists: _____

Please set up your document like this:
- One inch margins on all sides, SINGLE spaced.
- 12 point, simple font like Arial, Calibri, or Times New Roman.
- Cover page with your first and last name, period, and the interview title.
- Each question and answer should not have a blank space between them.
- New questions can have one space above them.
- Include an example of the artist's work on the last page and label it.
- Bibliography on the last page under the photo. (Every web address you got info from.)

Plagiarism & the use of A.I will result in a zero. Don't do it.

Please start your interview with an introduction; it's the polite thing to do. (And required) Something like this would be okay, but please give it your own twist.
I am pleased to present to you this interview with _____ who was born _____ and sadly died on _____. They worked in a style of art called _____ in the country of _____.

Pro Tip: Backwards Design Your Interview! In the gameshow Jeopardy, they give the players an answer, and they have to say the question. You can do the same thing, just write the answers as if it was a conversation.

From Wikipedia we read: *Born into an upper-middle-class family, Van Gogh drew as a child and was serious, quiet and thoughtful, but showed signs of mental instability. As a young man, he worked as an art dealer, often travelling, but became depressed after he was transferred to London. He turned to religion and spent time as a missionary in southern Belgium. Later he drifted into ill-health and solitude. He was keenly aware of modernist trends in art and, while back with his parents, took up painting in 1881. His younger brother, Theo, supported him financially, and the two of them maintained a long correspondence.*

What are some questions this text answers?

Q: _____

_____

Q: _____

_____

Possible Questions:

Answer questions in a paragraph form. Simple one-word or short answers are not acceptable! If an answer is shorter than a question, DON'T USE IT! Write as if it was a conversation, be creative and have fun, *but your facts must be true.*

IMPORTANT: *It is perfectly acceptable to expand on a fact and make it feel more "real" like in an interview, as long as it is based on real information. So in the example from Van Gogh, we know that his younger brother supported him financially. How do you think it feels for an older brother to depend on his younger brother for financial support? Answer the question with the fact, and then expand on it to make your interview feel more real and interesting like this:*

Q: Were you able to make a living doing your art?
V.G.: I actually had to depend on my little brother for financial support I am embarrassed to say. As an elder brother, I should be the one to carry on the family name and success. My little brother should look up to me for advice and help when necessary. To know that I only sold one work of art while I was alive, and I sold it to my brother is sad. No wonder I was depressed! It got so bad I had to be institutionalized.

The first 5 questions and the <u>LAST</u> are MANDATORY:
1. **Can you tell me a bit about your family and childhood?**
2. **What kinds of art do you like to create?**
3. **What do you think makes your work unique or special?**
4. **What is your most famous work of art?** *(Describe it, include a print-out at the end of the interview and label it with title, artist's name, material, size, and year.)*
5. **What was going on in the world when you were an artist?** *(Add 20 years to their birth year and find important historical event(s) they might have known about.)*
6. How did you die?
7. What other artists or styles influenced your work?
8. What did the people of YOUR TIME think of your work?
9. Does your art have a message or political point of view?
10. Did anything unusual happen to you as a kid?
11. Were you a religious person?
12. Did religion influence your work?
13. Did you always want to be an artist?
14. Who was your favorite artist or artists?
15. Did you have any friends who were artists too?
16. Did you do any other jobs besides being an artist?
17. Do you have any regrets?
18. Were you famous and successful in life?

19. Did you have a family of your own and were they supportive?
20. Were you ever in love? (Who?)
21. Did love or the lack of love influence your work?
22. How did people come to learn about you or your work?
23. Did you participate in any important exhibitions?
24. What museums have your work?
25. How much did your work sell for during your lifetime?
26. How much might some of your artwork sell for today?
27. How did you learn to be an artist?
28. Did you learn to make art on your own or go to school for it?
29. What is something interesting about yourself not related to your art?
30. What kind of student were you in school?
31. When did you first show signs of creativity?
32. What themes or ideas inspire your creativity?
33. Though you are known for your _____, what other kind of art did you do?
34. Did you have any influential teachers, mentors, or supporters?
35. Did you fit in with your friends and neighbors or were you an outcast?
36. How old were you when you started to become well known?
37. What do people say about your art today? (Look up critical reviews)
38. Is there a work of art you made that you do not like?
39. Did you have any pets?
40. Was there a work of art by another artist that influenced you?
41. Did you ever copy another work of art and do it in your own style?
42. Are there any artists that have stolen your art by remaking it in their style?
43. What was something really good that happened in your life?
44. What kinds of problems did you experience in your life?
45. What was something really bad that happened in your life?
46. Was there something in your life you had to overcome? (...and did you?)
47. If you could change something about your life, what would it be and why?
48. If you were living and working today as an artist, would it be easier or harder? (Why?)
49. What do you hope people learn from your art?
50. What do you want people to remember most about you?

LAST Mandatory Question: What words of wisdom would you like to end this interview with? (Include a real quote by artist. If you find none, include a quote by a museum about their work.)

Please grade your own project with the rubric below before you hand it in.

	100 Exceeds Expectations	**90** Meets all requirements	**80** Meets most requirements	**70** Meets some requirements	**60** Meets few requirements	**Zero** Little or no evidence
Completeness	Work went beyond expectations with significant additional length, info, materials, etc.	Work was the correct length and all required elements are met.	Work was about 10% shorter than required and/or a required element was missing.	Work was about 20 to 30% shorter than required and/or a few required elements were missing.	Work was more than 25% shorter than required and/or many required elements were missing.	Hardly anything was completed. Less than 25% of required work was done.
Formatting* • Margins/Fonts • cover page • introduction • labeled image • required length • websites cited • directions followed	All requirements were met and some exceeded with exceptional craftsmanship and creative touches.	All requirements were met. *(See list)	One required formatting element was missing or significantly deficient; like using a larger font, or wide spacing.	Two required formatting elements were missing or deficient like the use large fonts or wide spacing or margins to hide lack of content.	More than 2 required elements missing or significantly deficient. Little evidence formatting was thoughtful.	Most or all required elements missing or significantly deficient.
Originality	Unique, significantly artful, and/or an unexpected approach to the project that enhanced its overall presentation.	The project was original without derivative elements or work copied from others.	The work was fairly original with little that was copied or borrowed from the internet or other sources. All copied info was cited.	Some portions of the work appear to be copied from other sources but cited in the bibliography.	Portions of the work appear to be copied from other sources and not cited properly, but are not willful plagiarism, just carelessness.	Little appears to be the student's original work, and/or it includes significant plagiarism.
Depth of content	All portions of the work are focused, rich, and informative. Even creative elements add to its educational value.	The work was focused and on point. None was distracting or "filler." It provided good and insightful information about the artist.	Most of the work was focused and on point. Little was distracting or "filler." It provided some good information about the artist.	Some of the work was focused and on point. Some was distracting or "filler." It provided some information about the artist.	Little of the work was focused. Much of it seemed off topic or did not provide focused information about the artist and their work.	Off topic, incoherent, providing little or no meaningful content.
Grammar Spelling Organization Proofreading	Good editing & proofreading is obvious. No errors found. Work flows beautifully; it is well organized, and thoughtful. Professional feel.	Work is free of major spelling and grammar issues. The organization of thoughts is good and free of distractions.	Work could have been improved by proofreading and some errors could have been corrected. There are a few minor organizational issues.	Work contains many issues that could have been solved by some proofreading. The flow of ideas or organization is somewhat distracting.	Grammar and spelling contain significant issues. Little attempt at proofreading is evident making this project very difficult to read.	No attempt was made to proofread or organize content at all. Careless and unfocused.

Recorded Grade _____   Comments: _____

Art History "Story Time" Assignment.

Find 4-6 famous works of art that you feel "tell a story." You will use those images as illustrations for a story you will write. When complete, you will have at least ___ full pages of text (if all the images were removed). There will be an additional fact sheet to include which will bring the total writing requirement to 3 pages of text. **You can do more,** but doing less will impact your score/grade. See Rubric.

Each image will need to be labeled & numbered underneath to credit the artist like this below:

1. Starry Night by Vincent Van Gogh, oil on canvas, 1889, Style: Post Impressionism.
[Number, Title, Name of Artist, Material, Year, & Style]

Formatting:
- Single Spaced
- 12 point Arial or Times Font
- 1 empty line between paragraphs
- No indenting
- 1 inch margins all the way around.
- Cover page with title, name, & period does not count in the text requirement.
- Story should equal **AT LEAST** 2 full pages of text.

Image Selection:
- DO NOT use images/illustrations already used in stories/literature.
- Work must be from historically significant artists.
- You may use up to ONE image from a living artist who has work in at least one museum.
- You may use any other form of art like paintings, drawings, sculpture.
- Images DO NOT have to be from the same artist, style, material, theme. Mixing is okay.

Fact Sheet:
At the end of your writing, you will need to research and provide facts about the art and the artist you used for your images. Facts should be in complete sentences. Short or incomplete facts will not count.

- 3 Facts about each artwork
- 3 facts about the artist who made the artwork*
- *If one artist is used for 4 artworks, then you will have a total of 12 facts for that particular artist. (3 x 4 = 12) Choosing one artist does not simplify the writing requirement.

Pre-Planning:
Your writing needs to have 4 major components that will be assessed. *Write notes below.*

1. Characters: Who

2. Setting: Where, When

3. Plot: rising action – the story, the journey, leading to the climax – (The win, loss, or discovery)

4. Resolution: Stories do not need to have a happy ending, but they can.

5 Worksheet: Complete the worksheet on the next page. It is important to number your selected artworks so that everything stays in order. You may change selections if you find better images as you work, but erase and change your pre-work. This pre-work will provide evidence of your depth of knowledge. It is important to include it for the highest assessment possible.

Image Planning Sheet:

Create a simple sketch in each box. Label it. (4 minimum, 6 maximum)

1. Title, Year: Artist, Media:	2. Title, Year: Artist, Media:
3. Title, Year: Artist, Media:	4. Title, Year: Artist, Media:
5. Title, Year: Artist, Media:	6. Title, Year: Artist, Media:

Fact Sheet: (Facts must be full sentences/complete thoughts)

Artwork 1: *Title:* _____

Fact 1. _____
Fact 2. _____
Fact 3. _____

Artist *Name* _____

Fact 1. _____
Fact 2. _____
Fact 3. _____

Artwork 2: *Title:* _____

Fact 1. _____
Fact 2. _____
Fact 3. _____

Artist *Name* _____

Fact 1. _____
Fact 2. _____
Fact 3. _____

Artwork 3: *Title:* _____

Fact 1. _____
Fact 2. _____
Fact 3. _____

Artist *Name* _____

Fact 1. _____
Fact 2. _____
Fact 3. _____

Artwork 4: *Title:* _____

Fact 1. _____
Fact 2. _____
Fact 3. _____

Artist *Name* _____

Fact 1. _____
Fact 2. _____
Fact 3. _____

Please grade your own writing with the rubric below by underlining items.

	100 Exceeds Expectations	**90** Meets all requirements	**80** Meets most requirements	**70** Meets some requirements	**60** Meets few requirements	**Zero** Little or no evidence
Characters	Well considered and added layers of meaning to the story. Personal connections were also evident.	Characters all had purpose and served the story well.	Characters mostly had purpose but some were less resolved than others.	The characters seemed disconnected to the story and some served no real purpose to the plot.	Though present, they did not seem to be appropriate to the story. Disconnected and perhaps distracting.	Not well considered or included in the development of the story.
Setting	Well considered and added layers of meaning to the story. It was described in rich detail. Personal connections were also evident.	Environment had purpose and served the story well. Some details were included to liven the environment.	Environment had a purpose but less resolved or lacking details that would have made it feel more rich or real.	The environment seemed disconnected to the story and some served no real purpose to the plot.	Though present, it did not seem to be appropriate to the story. Disconnected and perhaps distracting.	Not well considered or included in the development of the story.
Plot	ORIGNIAL and well considered and added layers of meaning to the story. It engaged the reader the entire time with unique details or twists with purpose.	Fairly original and well considered. It engaged the reader most of the time. The actions served the story well and made sense.	A bit derivative (*based on another story*) but well considered. It engaged the reader some of the time. The sequence made sense.	The plot seemed derivative, or lacked originality, or had confusing plot-holes, but the sequence of events mostly made sense.	The plot was difficult to follow and was missing important details to help the reader understand the sequence of events.	Not well considered or included in the development of the story.
Resolution	Well considered and meaningful to the story. It was described in rich detail with a deeper message. Personal connections and point of view were also evident.	The ending had purpose and served the story well. There was a message or moral purpose in the end.	The ending had a purpose but less resolved or lacking details that would have made it feel connected or purposeful.	The ending seemed disconnected to the story and not well tied to the purpose of the plot.	The ending did not seem to be connected to the story. Disconnected and perhaps distracting.	Not well considered or included in the development of the story.
Formatting & connected to selected artworks.	Exceeded the required length. Good editing & proof-reading. Work flows beautifully. Art choices feel naturally & fully integrated into the story in the details.	Met the required length & formatting. Proofreading is evident in the lack of common errors. Artwork is solidly connected to the story.	Missed length or formatting details. Work could have been improved by proofreading. The selected images are connected to the story though loosely.	Missed length & formatting details. Proofreading would have helped. The images lack strong connections to the story.	Too short and not formatted. Lack of proofreading is evident. The images are not well connected to the story but are included.	No attempt was made to proofread or organize content at all. Careless and unfocused use of images.
Fact Sheet	More than 3 facts ea. about the artist &/or artwork(s)	3 facts ea. about the artist & artwork	2 facts missing or short.	4 facts missing or short	Many facts missing or short	No fact sheet

Recorded Grade _____ Comments _____

_____

Schools Of Art - Introduction

Let's find out more about the schools of art. Using textbooks, the internet, or library. Try to complete as much of this information as you can.

1. Renaissance: Dates:_____

Definition:

What is special or unique about this school of art?

Two Artists: _____ & _____

2. Baroque: Dates: _____

Definition:

What is special or unique about this school of art?

Two Artists: _____ & _____

3. Rococo: Dates: _____

Definition:

What is special or unique about this school of art?

Two Artists: _____ & _____

4. Neo-Classical: Dates: _____

Definition:

What is special or unique about this school of art?

Two Artists: _____ & _____

5. Romanticism: Dates: _____

Definition:

What is special or unique about this school of art?

Two Artists: _____ & _____

6. Realism : Dates _____

Definition:

What is special or unique about this school of art?

Two Artists: _____ & _____

7. Impressionism : Dates _____

Definition:

What is special or unique about this school of art?

Two Artists: _____ & _____

8. Expressionism: Dates _____

Definition:

What is special or unique about this school of art?

Two Artists: _____ & _____

9. Cubism: Date _____ (*This one is an exact year*)

Definition:

What is special or unique about this school of art?

Two Artists: _____ & _____

10. Dada: Dates _____

Definition:

What is special or unique about this school of art?

Two Artists: _____ & _____

11. Surrealism: Dates _____

Definition:

What is special or unique about this school of art?

Two Artists: _____ & _____

12. Abstract Expressionism: Dates _____

Definition:

What is special or unique about this school of art?

Two Artists: _____ & _____

13. Pop art: Dates _____

Definition:

What is special or unique about this school of art?

Two Artists: _____ & _____

14. What style seems the most interesting and why?

_____

_____

_____

15. What painting did you see that you liked the most and why?

_____

_____

_____

Schools of Art Overview
Write 3 facts about each.

Renaissance
1. _____
2. _____
3. _____

Baroque
1. _____
2. _____
3. _____

Rococo
1. _____
2. _____
3. _____

Neo-Classical
1. _____
2. _____
3. _____

Romanticism
1. _____
2. _____
3. _____

Realism
1. _____
2. _____
3. _____

Impressionism
1. _____
2. _____
3. _____

Cubism
1. _____
2. _____
3. _____

Dada
1. _____
2. _____
3. _____

Surrealism
1. _____
2. _____
3. _____

Expressionism
1. _____
2. _____
3. _____

Abstract Expressionism
1. _____
2. _____
3. _____

Pop Art
1. _____
2. _____
3. _____

Tutorials: https://bit.ly/SchoolsOfArt

Schools of Art List
Video Support: https://bit.ly/SchoolsOfArt

Renaissance – French word for "rebirth," This work showed Greek, Roman or Bible stories, they tried to make the work look 3-D with perspective. It is the oldest style we need to know, and looks old. Some artists would include Leonardo da Vinci, Michelangelo, (and the other Ninja Turtles. 1400-1500s

Baroque – Looks like it might be on stage and have a spotlight. Look for drama in the action or the lighting. Often has very dark and very light areas, but not always. You might see Musketeer's style clothes of the 1600s.

Rococo – Sickeningly Sweet, everything is rosy and RICH, it shows people playing. Cute and fluffy were their main ideas. Rococo is like Baroque but topped off with a tub of sugar. Look for Cinderella style dresses. Early 1700s

Neo-Classical –Rococo's opposite. The Neo-Classical artists were trying to kick out the King and queen. The paintings are VERY organized, serious, often with big shapes hidden in the paintings. These paintings often included Greek and Roman images so be careful to not confuse it with Renaissance. Most buildings in Washington DC are examples of this style. During the French and American revolutions.

Romanticism – In the early 1800s, it usually showed man and nature but not always peaceful. Sometimes man is using nature—like hills or mountains to fight a war, or hunt to feed his family, but man is never hurting nature in this work, the opposite may be true. If images include slaves, it's probably the next style...

Realism –Is what it sounds like. Realism showed the good and the bad. It began before there were cameras, so the artists tried to paint as much detail as they could. Today, some of these paintings look like photographs. Before, people were usually painted prettier than they were. Middle 1800s

Impressionism – Started in France in the 1860's, the artists tried to paint to show how

Cont...
important light is. Monet, Cassatt, Van Gogh, Cézanne, and Pissaro are Impressionist painters These paintings are usually THICK with paint. Paintings are made while looking at what you are painting. Many of these paintings have a "Z" pattern hiding inside them. Late 1800s

Cubism – Started by Pablo Picasso with his painting in 1907 of Demoiselles d'Avignon. Usually the art looks shattered, and broken into shapes like broken glass, but you can still see what's going on.
NOT ALL work with shapes is CUBISM!

Expressionism – These paintings must have images you can understand but it is a little weird, or very strange to express emotions. All art should show emotion, the artists of this school of art use color or shape to help make the emotions stand out. Edvard Munch is an artist of this style. 1920s

Abstract Expressionism – NO pictures can be seen. The work looks like splashes, or layers of color, or child-like. *If you can't tell at all what's going on in the painting it is probably this style.* 1940s

Dada – A strange art movement that started in Germany in the early 1920's. The artists tried to make fun of art and the people who liked museum art. They would make things that most people thought was junk, or not "real" art, like a toilet up-side-down. Marcel DuChamp is a famous artist of this style. 1920s

Surrealism – Started in the 1920's and was often about dreams or the secrets in your brain. Art in the Surrealist style often looked dreamlike or impossible. Some artists were De Chirico, Salvador Dali, Rene Magritte, and Joan Míro.

Pop Art – Started in New York in the 1950s and 60s, a style of art that comes from popular culture including stuff you buy in a store (like soup or soda), commercials, simple every-day stuff, and cartoons. Some famous artists Keith Haring, Claes Oldenburg, and Andy Warhol.

Important art to remember

Pablo Picasso, **1907** of *Demoiselles d'Avignon*.

The painting above is the first painting in human history that a person was painted in a way that was different on purpose. They style is called Cubism, it was the first one! **Below** is the *Mona Lisa*, by Leonardo Da Vinci, a Renaissance Artist from the late 1400s. It is the most famous painting in the world!

The painting to the right →
…is a painting of a dream. The stuff in the painting is not real, but it is painted to look very real. This is called surrealism.

Starry Night, by Vincent VanGogh,

The painting above is special too, because the artist starts to use color to express his feelings. It is an Impressionist painting but some people call it post-impressionism.

Christina's World (above) by Andrew Wyeth is an example of Realism. It shows a lot of detail, and had both good things and bad things in the painting. People think it is a young girl, but it is really older lady named… Christina.

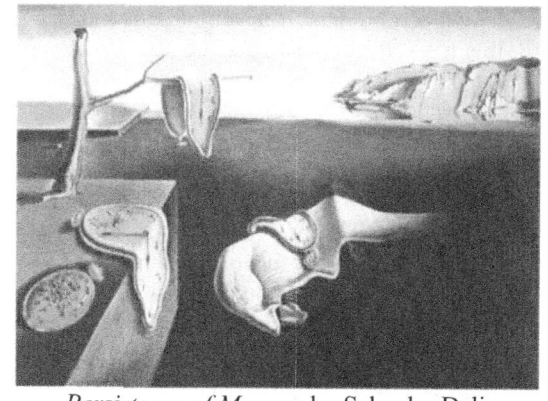

Persistence of Memory by Salvador Dali

Art History Flowchart

START HERE				
Is there a subject? Can you see "stuff" you recognize?	No	Check the title, are you sure there is no subject?	Yes	**Abstract Expressionism**
			No	Start Over
Yes				
Are people wearing togas? (*Roman Robes or capes*) If there are nudes, do they look like the kind you might see in church art?	Yes	Are their poses relaxed or very dramatic?	Relaxed	**Renaissance**
			Dramatic	**Neoclassical**
No				
Is there anything impossible, magical, or "dream-like" happening?	Yes	**Surrealism**		
No				
Is there a strong sense of emotion in the art and do the colors, shapes, or textures help make that stronger? **OR** does it have a very unusual use of shape, form, color, or texture that almost hides the subject?	Yes	Do you see obvious geometric shapes or shattered images?	Yes	**Cubism**
			No	**Expressionism**
No				
Does it include images from popular culture of regular common stuff with bold color that wouldn't normally be considered art?	Yes	Did it take effort to make?	Yes	**Pop Art**
			No	**Dada**
No				
Does it show very rich or royal people playing or being naughty? Do even the trees and clothes look rich and fluffy?	Yes	**Rococo**		
No				
Is the background very dark but you see dramatic spot-lighting? Is it old fashioned with clothing of the 1600s like from the 3 Musketeers or Pirates of the Caribbean	Yes	**Baroque**		
No				
Is the paint thick and obvious and could it have been painted from observation?	Yes	**Impressionism**		
No				
Do you see hunting, hiking, or farming? (People formally interacting with nature)	Yes	Are the people slaves, or are they looking at us?	Yes	**Realism**
			No	**Romanticism**
No				
Is it dramatic with an old battle on the land, or is nature overwhelming people?	Yes	**Romanticism**		
No				
Is something from nature hurting people or is it dramatic?	Yes	**Realism**		
It might be a style not on this chart.				

www.FirehousePublications.com

Schools of Art: Matching

Circle the description and draw a line to the image it belongs to.

Baroque: Highly organized and posed; Dramatic lighting like a spotlight: Older style but people wear the clothes of their time. People are not made to look better than they really are, so it's a bit more realistic. Musketeer style clothing.

Neoclassical: Highly organized and dramatic. Often includes a morality message. Created to look grand and important. People in the images often wear togas.

Renaissance: People in these images often wear togas but have relaxed poses. Though organized it is less dramatic than the other styles above. Often include themes from the Bible or mythology. Sometimes has hints of perspective.

Rococo: Usually includes images of the royalty of the time or the very rich. People in the images are often just playing or being a bit naughty. There is no morality message except to have fun. Trees and elements in the pictures have an overly "fluffy" appearance. Sickeningly sweet.

Circle the description and draw a line to the image it belongs to.

Dada: Art that looks the least like "ART." Sometimes considered absurd or an insult to art. Sometimes artists used simple common objects or random objects to be their art. It was very controversial but was a springboard for Pop Art which came later and is sometimes called *Neo-Dada*.

Romanticism: *NOT* about love, but the idea of man and nature together. Sometimes nature dominates man, and sometimes they coexist harmoniously. Man NEVER dominates nature in these images.

Realism: Is as it sounds, realistic. Images are created with attention to detail and showing things as they really are with their flaws and beauty. Sometimes this work has obvious brushstrokes, sometimes not. If it looks like a photograph it is likely this style or another called "photo-realism."

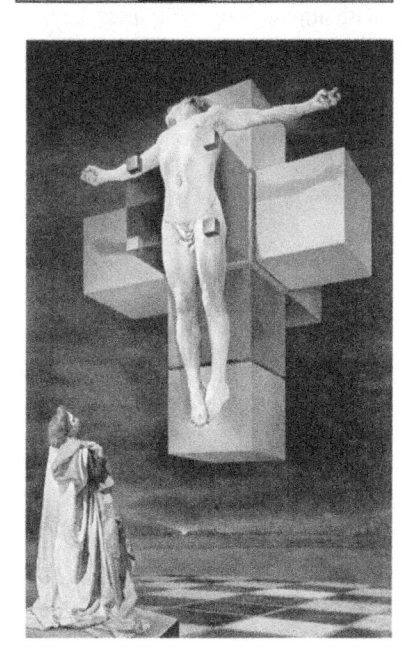

Circle the description and draw a line to the image it belongs to.

Surrealism: Sometimes very realistic but somehow impossible or dream-like. The style was developed based on psychological examination of dreams and symbols. Some of the work can be humorous, others can be haunting.

Pop Art: Generally colors are bold and vibrant. Images may be based on commercial products, common objects, cartoons, or images from popular culture. It is sometimes called *Neo-Dada*.

Cubism: Images often look shattered or reinterpreted with a geometric look. The subject is generally evident but is abstracted.

Circle the description and draw a line to the image it belongs to.

Abstract Expressionism: NO RECOGNIZABLE IMAGERY CAN BE SEEN. The meaning of the painting is derived from the colors, shapes, textures, or other art elements that the artist has chosen to manipulate. If you see something in the image, like an actual object (cat, cup, person) IT IS NOT THIS STYLE.

Expressionism: The artist uses one or more art elements *(color, shape, form…)* to express heightened emotions in the work. Joy, Anger, Pain, Love are some typical themes. In this style the subject can be easily seen though it may be a bit abstracted because of the expressive technique.

Impressionism: Concerned with the changing effects of light and depicting light. The work often includes bold brush strokes and textures. Sometimes a "Z" pattern can be seen within the work. Images are usually created from observation. Many paintings were created outdoors, but there are portraits, still lives, and more in this style.

Though strictly speaking Van Gogh was a Post Impressionist, in a pre-college level art class it is helpful to express him as an Impressionist as he displays the key qualities of Impressionism in an exaggerated way.

151

ABSTRACT is a term to mean "changed from reality." This can be slight or dramatic. *__Abstract is NOT a school of art, but a vocabulary term.__* When paired with expressionism it means the work has no visually recognizable imagery. Abstraction can be slight to extreme; we can see this below.

Realistic Photo   Slight Abstraction   Strong Abstraction   VERY Abstracted

REMEMBER, if there is a subject, then the art is based on a real thing, and it cannot be abstract expressionism. How about below? Is there a subject?

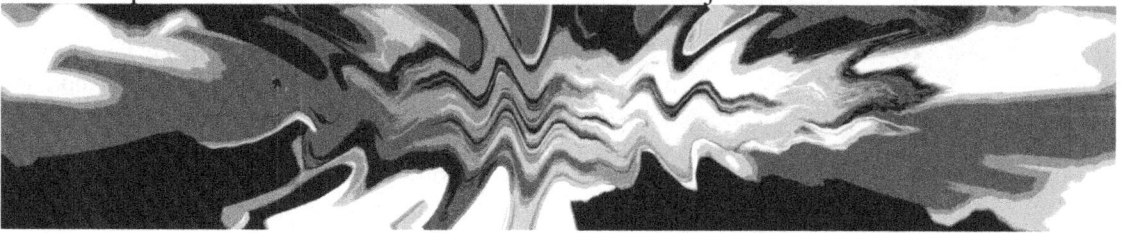

Your teacher will be able to show you many famous painting samples. Decide what school of art they belong to based on clues you see within the artwork.

Sketch Below: What school of art do you believe it to be from?

_____

What 3 pieces of evidence can you see?

1. _____

2. _____

3. _____

What was the real answer?

_____
If you were wrong, what did you miss?

_____

Sketch Below:

What school of art do you believe it to be from?

_____

What 3 pieces of evidence can you see?

1. _____

2. _____

3. _____

What was the real answer?

_____

If you were wrong, what did you miss?

Sketch Below:

What school of art do you believe it to be from?

_____

What 3 pieces of evidence can you see?

1. _____

2. _____

3. _____

What was the real answer?

_____

If you were wrong, what did you miss?

Sketch Below: What school of art do you believe it to be from?

_____

What 3 pieces of evidence can you see?

1. _____

2. _____

3. _____

What was the real answer?

_____

If you were wrong, what did you miss?

Sketch Below: What school of art do you believe it to be from?

_____

What 3 pieces of evidence can you see?

1. _____

2. _____

3. _____

What was the real answer?

_____

If you were wrong, what did you miss?

Sketch Below:

What school of art do you believe it to be from?

_____

What 3 pieces of evidence can you see?

1. _____

2. _____

3. _____

What was the real answer?

_____

If you were wrong, what did you miss?

Sketch Below:

What school of art do you believe it to be from?

_____

What 3 pieces of evidence can you see?

1. _____

2. _____

3. _____

What was the real answer?

_____

If you were wrong, what did you miss?

Sketch Below:

What school of art do you believe it to be from?

_____

What 3 pieces of evidence can you see?

1. _____

2. _____

3. _____

What was the real answer?

_____

If you were wrong, what did you miss?

Sketch Below:

What school of art do you believe it to be from?

_____

What 3 pieces of evidence can you see?

1. _____

2. _____

3. _____

What was the real answer?

_____

If you were wrong, what did you miss?

_____

Sketch Below: What school of art do you believe it to be from?

_____

What 3 pieces of evidence can you see?

1. _____

2. _____

3. _____

What was the real answer?

_____

If you were wrong, what did you miss?

Sketch Below: What school of art do you believe it to be from?

_____

What 3 pieces of evidence can you see?

1. _____

2. _____

3. _____

What was the real answer?

_____

If you were wrong, what did you miss?

Sketch Below:	What school of art do you believe it to be from?

_____

What 3 pieces of evidence can you see?

1. _____

2. _____

3. _____

What was the real answer?

_____

If you were wrong, what did you miss?

_____

Sketch Below:	What school of art do you believe it to be from?

_____

What 3 pieces of evidence can you see?

1. _____

2. _____

3. _____

What was the real answer?

_____

If you were wrong, what did you miss?

_____

Reflection/Closure

Date: _____ : _____

Date: _____ : _____

Date: _____ : _____

Date: _____ : _____

Date: _____ : _____

Date: _____ : _____

Date: _____ : _____

Date: _____ : _____

Date: _____ : _____

Date: _____ : _____

Date: _____ : _____

Date: _____ : _____

Date: _____ : _____

Date: _____ : _____

Date: _____ : _____

Date: _____ : _____

Date: _____ : _____

Date: _____ : _____

Date: _____ : _____

Reflection/Closure

Date: _____ : _____

Date: _____ : _____

Date: _____ : _____

Date: _____ : _____

Date: _____ : _____

Date: _____ : _____

Date: _____ : _____

Date: _____ : _____

Date: _____ : _____

Date: _____ : _____

Date: _____ : _____

Date: _____ : _____

Date: _____ : _____

Date: _____ : _____

Date: _____ : _____

Date: _____ : _____

Date: _____ : _____

Date: _____ : _____

Date: _____ : _____

Video Notes

Video notes are an essential part of your grade and the easiest "A's" you will ever earn... Sometimes the teacher will be here for these videos, BUT a teacher does not need to be here to push "play" on a DVD. These assignments are mostly given when the teacher is out of school for a conference or something. These assignments are to help you learn about Art History, a mandatory part of all art classes.

The teacher could assign readings within a textbook and written assignments... or you could do a video once in a while...

To earn your 100% all you need is 20 facts about what you see. They can be things you hear the artist or moderator say, but they can also be things you observe in the video. Mainly the teacher needs to see evidence that you have watched the video and paid attention. **Two word facts are NOT acceptable.** Most students can get all the notes before the video is even half over. There is no excuse for not completing these assignments and getting 100%.

IF you are absent for the video, you will be excused from the assignment. Your name MUST appear as absent on the school's attendance roster. You may use a "Pass Point" instead of doing the notes, but this is a waste of a VALUABLE opportunity to raise a test grade. You will never be pestered into doing these assignments... it is after all, your own grade.

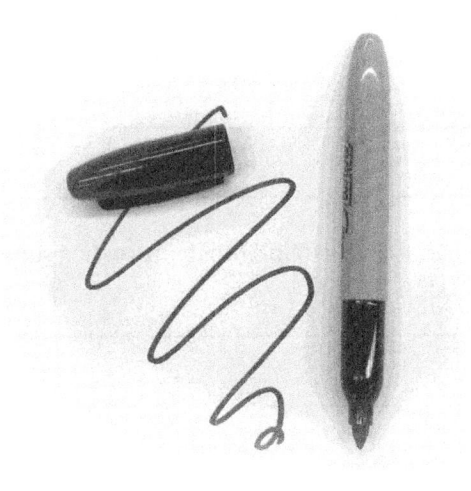

Short Video Notes (Vimo/Youtube)   **Title or Topic** _____

Note 5 facts or interesting observations about the video.

1. _____
2. _____
3. _____
4. _____
5. _____

　　　Reflecting on the video, what did you find most interesting, unique, or thought provoking?

_____
_____
_____

- -

Short Video Notes (Vimo/Youtube)   **Title or Topic** _____

Note 5 facts or interesting observations about the video.

1. _____
2. _____
3. _____
4. _____
5. _____

　　　Reflecting on the video, what did you find most interesting, unique, or thought provoking?

_____
_____
_____

Short Video Notes (Vimo/Youtube)   **Title or Topic** _____

Note 5 facts or interesting observations about the video.

1. _____
2. _____
3. _____
4. _____
5. _____

      Reflecting on the video, what did you find most interesting, unique, or thought provoking?

_____

_____

_____

- -

Short Video Notes (Vimo/Youtube)   **Title or Topic** _____

Note 5 facts or interesting observations about the video.

1. _____
2. _____
3. _____
4. _____
5. _____

      Reflecting on the video, what did you find most interesting, unique, or thought provoking?

_____

_____

_____

Short Video Notes (Vimo/Youtube)   **Title or Topic** _____

Note 5 facts or interesting observations about the video.

1. _____
2. _____
3. _____
4. _____
5. _____

Reflecting on the video, what did you find most interesting, unique, or thought provoking?

_____
_____
_____

Short Video Notes (Vimo/Youtube)   **Title or Topic** _____

Note 5 facts or interesting observations about the video.

1. _____
2. _____
3. _____
4. _____
5. _____

Reflecting on the video, what did you find most interesting, unique, or thought provoking?

_____
_____
_____

Short Video Notes (Vimo/Youtube)   **Title or Topic** _____

Note 5 facts or interesting observations about the video.

1. _____

2. _____

3. _____

4. _____

5. _____

Reflecting on the video, what did you find most interesting, unique, or thought provoking?

_____

_____

_____

Short Video Notes (Vimo/Youtube)   **Title or Topic** _____

Note 5 facts or interesting observations about the video.

1. _____

2. _____

3. _____

4. _____

5. _____

Reflecting on the video, what did you find most interesting, unique, or thought provoking?

_____

_____

_____

VIDEO NOTES – GRADED ASSIGNMENT

TITLE_____ Period____ Date __/__/__

Directions: Write 20 facts below based on the video WHILE YOU WATCH. **Two word facts, silliness, and incomplete thoughts will not be acceptable.** *This is GRADED as part of 10% of your quarter's grade.*

1. _____
2. _____
3. _____
4. _____
5. _____
6. _____
7. _____
8. _____
9. _____
10. _____
11. _____
12. _____
13. _____
14. _____
15. _____
16. _____
17. _____
18. _____
19. _____
20. _____

Summarize the video. What is the main idea or what can you infer? (10 pts.)
_____
_____
_____

Double check that all facts have MORE than 2 words.

GRADED BY TEACHER: FULL CREDIT 100%   OR _____% Credit

VIDEO NOTES – GRADED ASSIGNMENT

TITLE_____ Period___ Date __/__/__

Directions: Write 20 facts below based on the video WHILE YOU WATCH. **Two word facts, silliness, and incomplete thoughts will not be acceptable.** *This is GRADED as part of 10% of your quarter's grade.*

1. _____
2. _____
3. _____
4. _____
5. _____
6. _____
7. _____
8. _____
9. _____
10. _____
11. _____
12. _____
13. _____
14. _____
15. _____
16. _____
17. _____
18. _____
19. _____
20. _____

Summarize the video. What is the main idea or what can you infer? (10 pts.)
_____
_____
_____

Double check that all facts have MORE than 2 words.

GRADED BY TEACHER: FULL CREDIT 100%   OR _____% Credit

VIDEO NOTES – GRADED ASSIGNMENT

TITLE_____ Period____ Date __/__/__

Directions: Write 20 facts below based on the video WHILE YOU WATCH. **Two word facts, silliness, and incomplete thoughts will not be acceptable.** *This is GRADED as part of 10% of your quarter's grade.*

1. _____
2. _____
3. _____
4. _____
5. _____
6. _____
7. _____
8. _____
9. _____
10. _____
11. _____
12. _____
13. _____
14. _____
15. _____
16. _____
17. _____
18. _____
19. _____
20. _____

Summarize the video. What is the main idea or what can you infer? (10 pts.)
_____
_____
_____

Double check that all facts have MORE than 2 words.

GRADED BY TEACHER: FULL CREDIT 100%   OR _____% Credit

VIDEO NOTES – GRADED ASSIGNMENT

TITLE_____ Period____ Date __/__/__

Directions: Write 20 facts below based on the video WHILE YOU WATCH. **Two word facts, silliness, and incomplete thoughts will not be acceptable.** *This is GRADED as part of 10% of your quarter's grade.*

1. _____
2. _____
3. _____
4. _____
5. _____
6. _____
7. _____
8. _____
9. _____
10. _____
11. _____
12. _____
13. _____
14. _____
15. _____
16. _____
17. _____
18. _____
19. _____
20. _____

Summarize the video. What is the main idea or what can you infer? (10 pts.)
_____
_____
_____

Double check that all facts have MORE than 2 words.

GRADED BY TEACHER: FULL CREDIT 100%   OR _____% Credit

VIDEO NOTES – GRADED ASSIGNMENT

TITLE_____ Period___ Date __/__/__

Directions: Write 20 facts below based on the video WHILE YOU WATCH. **Two word facts, silliness, and incomplete thoughts will not be acceptable.** *This is GRADED as part of 10% of your quarter's grade.*

1. _____
2. _____
3. _____
4. _____
5. _____
6. _____
7. _____
8. _____
9. _____
10. _____
11. _____
12. _____
13. _____
14. _____
15. _____
16. _____
17. _____
18. _____
19. _____
20. _____

Summarize the video. What is the main idea or what can you infer? (10 pts.)
_____
_____
_____

Double check that all facts have MORE than 2 words.

GRADED BY TEACHER: FULL CREDIT 100%   OR _____% Credit

VIDEO NOTES – GRADED ASSIGNMENT

TITLE_____ Period___ Date __/__/__

Directions: Write 20 facts below based on the video WHILE YOU WATCH. **Two word facts, silliness, and incomplete thoughts will not be acceptable.** *This is GRADED as part of 10% of your quarter's grade.*

1. _____
2. _____
3. _____
4. _____
5. _____
6. _____
7. _____
8. _____
9. _____
10. _____
11. _____
12. _____
13. _____
14. _____
15. _____
16. _____
17. _____
18. _____
19. _____
20. _____

Summarize the video. What is the main idea or what can you infer? (10 pts.)
_____
_____
_____

Double check that all facts have MORE than 2 words.

GRADED BY TEACHER: FULL CREDIT 100% OR _____% Credit

VIDEO NOTES – GRADED ASSIGNMENT

TITLE_____ Period____ Date __/__/__

Directions: Write 20 facts below based on the video WHILE YOU WATCH. **Two word facts, silliness, and incomplete thoughts will not be acceptable.** *This is GRADED as part of 10% of your quarter's grade.*

1. _____
2. _____
3. _____
4. _____
5. _____
6. _____
7. _____
8. _____
9. _____
10. _____
11. _____
12. _____
13. _____
14. _____
15. _____
16. _____
17. _____
18. _____
19. _____
20. _____

Summarize the video. What is the main idea or what can you infer? (10 pts.)
_____
_____
_____

Double check that all facts have MORE than 2 words.

GRADED BY TEACHER: FULL CREDIT 100%   OR _____ % Credit

VIDEO NOTES – GRADED ASSIGNMENT

TITLE_____ Period____ Date __/__/__

Directions: Write 20 facts below based on the video WHILE YOU WATCH. **Two word facts, silliness, and incomplete thoughts will not be acceptable.** *This is GRADED as part of 10% of your quarter's grade.*

1. _____
2. _____
3. _____
4. _____
5. _____
6. _____
7. _____
8. _____
9. _____
10. _____
11. _____
12. _____
13. _____
14. _____
15. _____
16. _____
17. _____
18. _____
19. _____
20. _____

Summarize the video. What is the main idea or what can you infer? (10 pts.)
_____
_____
_____

Double check that all facts have MORE than 2 words.

GRADED BY TEACHER: FULL CREDIT 100%   OR _____ % Credit

SKETCHBOOK IDEAS

If you finish a project early, or will be at home for an extended period of time, these are some simple assignments you can complete on your own.

Baseline Drawing 1: Draw a shoe in as much detail as you can.

Baseline drawing 2: Draw yourself in a mirror with as much detail as you can.

Baseline Drawing 3: Draw your hand in as much detail as you can.

Fill a page with scribbles, and then look at them and reveal what can be seen in them. This is similar to looking at clouds and spotting objects in them, but here you color them in.

Rip a random small piece of paper from a magazine and draw it. Enlarge it to fill the page.

Draw the view through a window.

Write your name 30 times, in different sizes and directions, overlapping often to divide the page into many shapes. Color in using colors that express your mood today using the expressive colors and shapes worksheet.

Draw a tree from your imagination then draw a tree from observation. Which looks better to you? Why?

Trace your hand in an interesting position and turn it into an animal. DO NOT MAKE A TURKEY.

Find a common small object and enlarge it to fill your paper.

Draw yourself in a mirror but DO NOT look at the paper while you do it.

Draw a friend or family member with one continuous line. Do not lift the pencil until it is complete.

Find a tree and draw what is seen between the branches without drawing the tree itself.

Find a face in a magazine or photograph, turn it up-side-down and draw it up-side-down too.

Fill a page with shapes, get into every corner, but DO NOT lift your pencil until you are done. Color in using colors that express your personality using the expressive colors and shapes worksheet.

Draw some clouds from observation.

Draw your hand holding a CD. Draw as much of yourself in the mirror as you can see even if it is just a fragment.

Trace a leaf, trace the shadow it makes. Color in as realistically as you can like trompe l'oeil.

Trace your hand in an interesting position; fill it with patterns and color that express what you like to do with your hands.

Draw what you have in your pockets right now.

Draw a shoe, position the laces in such a way as to create a hidden face in your show. Draw it realistically but be sure to capture the idea of a face as well.

Take 2 unrelated objects and create a hybrid image of this new object. (Like scissors and a bird)

Spy on someone and draw them without them knowing.

Draw your meal or utensils.

Half fill a clear glass with water. Place 1 or 2 objects inside that are both in and out of the liquid (like a spoon or chopstick), draw it.

Take a common object that would relate to yourself, then repeat that object to make an animal that you also feel expresses your personality. Feel free to abstract and stretch the objects to make your animal.

Get a new pencil, do a drawing of something around you by holding the very end where the eraser is.

Write your name and a short statement in block letters, maybe a poem or memory, BUT do it with your eyes closed. Color in after you are done.

Using only color and shape, try to do a drawing that represents LOVE without using a heart.

Do a drawing of the feeling of WAR with colors and shapes and NO objects. Try other words.

Do a hybrid drawing of 2 unrelated animals as a new animal (lion & fish maybe). Be sure to have examples of both in front of you if possible.

Try to draw an object from observation as if you were looking at it through a shattered window or mirror.

Draw an object from observation but draw several points of view at the same time, overlapping.

Try to draw a moving object and capture the idea of that movement you observe.

Take a magazine image, cut it in half and paste onto a new paper. (Rubber cement works best) Complete the missing half by hand. Include shadows too.

Take the magazine image left over from the last drawing and paste on another sheet of paper. Complete the missing half in a strange and unexpected way.

Draw a childhood memory.

Using a reference like yourself, a friend, or picture, draw a detailed eye.

Draw the line that separates your lips. Note how dynamic this line really is. Finish by adding your upper and lower lips.

Draw a night scene from observation through a widow.

Draw a unique dragon.

Gargoyles are meant to protect you and scare away evil spirits. Draw and create your own gargoyle to keep one of your fears away from you. For example, if you have a fear of darkness, your gargoyle might hold a torch or emit light.

Find an un-illustrated poem & create a picture for it.

Draw a solid object from observation, but do it as if it were glass.

Tightly wrap an object with cloth. Be sure the form of the object can still be understood. Draw It.

Fill a page with an image that simulates the texture of rock. Have a rock as reference to look at.

Draw a coin but enlarge it to fill the page. Add shadows and shines to make it look 3-D.

Draw a still life with 5 objects but color them with the opposite colors than they actually are.

Draw the outline of an observed object. Create a negative by coloring highlights, dark shadows, and areas of light.

Set two very differently colored and textured objects side by side, but color & texture one with the colors & textures of its neighbor.

Draw the outlines of two objects and partially overlap the drawings. Color each with a different primary color, where they overlap color with the secondary color they would create.

Color in a whole page with gray, use an eraser to draw. Try to vary the tones you see. Finish by adding very dark tones with heavy pencil. Be sure erasures show.

Draw something as if you were losing your mind.

Create a black and white landscape with one object in color.

Sketch a new way to design the face of a clock.

Write a short poem backwards (Mirror Writing) with big bold overlapping block letters. Color in the spaces created with analogous colors (Neighboring Colors on the color wheel)

Create a cartoon of yourself or a friend.

Draw a portrait of a friend or yourself; color in by signing that person's name over and over. Layer names for shadows like crosshatching.

Draw a self portrait made entirely of objects that represent what interests you.

Create a logo for yourself; be sure that it contains a clue about your personality.

Draw yourself as a monster.

Set an object in a box. Draw the object in the box; include the inside of the box in your drawing.

Draw an outline of a simple object.
- Draw the object again without lifting your pencil.
- Draw the object again without looking at your hand while you draw. Try to do it with a mostly continuous line.
- Draw the object's outline and shade with crosshatching lines.
- Draw the object again and use scribble lines to create shadow.
- Draw the object again only using dots for color and shadow.

Take a pattered fabric or shirt, drape it over a chair and draw it showing the pattern changes as the fabric folds and drapes.

Draw an object from observation above. Color the light side with warm colors (yellow through red) and the shaded side with cool colors like purple, blue, and green.

Put together a group of similarly colored objects. Set them up on a contrasting or opposite color for a still life drawing.

Draw a flag that would represent your family. Try to be symbolic. Use the worksheet in this book on the expressive qualities of shapes and colors.

Draw something from an unusual point of view.

Draw your hand drawing your hand in a funny way. (M.C. Escher did something like this)

Find a small simple, common object. Draw it large and turn it into an architectural design.

Draw your head realistically or as a cartoon. Add a large hole or opening to it and have objects escaping from that hole that tell a story about what goes on in your mind.

Trace an object about the size of this page, onto a page. Turn it into a very different object by how you finish the drawing. A pair of scissors may become a bird. You may add onto the object as you wish, try not to erase much of the original outline.

Cover half of your face with an object, and then create a self portrait.

Draw an original super hero with a power you wish you had.

Draw a stabbed object. (Like a piece of fruit with a pencil stabbed into it) Make the drawing with exaggerated sense of emotion.

Draw someone talking. Fill the background with their words in a creative way. This could be a historical figure or someone around you today.

Draw something flying that would not normally be able to fly.

Write an expressive word in large fat bubble-letters. Fill in the letters with images that relate the meaning of the word.

Draw an animal based on a photograph of it, BUT only draw it with letters found in its name. It is okay to abstract the letters to make them fit. Use the colors of the animal to finish it.

Design an item of clothing, color and texture it.

Draw the kind of house you would like to live in.

Draw your hand pointed away from you toward an object, draw both your hand and the object. Overlap a bit if you can to add realism and a hint of perspective.

Use candles, burn sticks and draw a still life with home-made charcoal.

Draw a wall with windows, and details of adjacent items like bookshelves, chairs, etc. Then draw an unexpected environment through the window.

Draw yours or a friend's face, divide it into 4 parts, and color each section with symbols for 4 things that are important to that person.

Trace your hand and draw what might be inside if you were an awesome robot.

Paste down half a face from a magazine. Choose an attractive model. Finish the other half of the face as if they were an alien.

If you could design your very own cell phone, what would it look like?

Draw a container, and on the back draw something unexpected that would be inside the container. Hold the page up to the light to see an x-ray view of both.

Design a piece of jewelry and use a symbol from your own cultural background in it.

Draw a piece of foil with a few wrinkles in it.

Place a coin under a page, rub a pencil over the page to create an embossed image. Then draw your hand holding the coin.

Draw a design you think would make a cool tattoo for you. Remember that tattoos are often symbolic of thing important to the person wearing it.

Draw the *thing* that lives under a child's bed.

Draw someone's ear from about 6 inches away from them. Be so close you can see every detail.

Using a flashlight, draw an object and its shades and highlights, but light it from an unusual point of view. (Like a face with the light below the chin, or still life lit from below.

Crumple a page, flatten it lightly so the creases are still obvious, then draw the page.

Draw a CD cover for your favorite song.

Draw your home as a castle but include details that are there right now.

Crumple this page, lightly flatten it, and trace the wrinkles making what you can imagine into the creases. This is similar to finding objects in clouds. As you stare, object will become apparent.

Draw something dry as if it was wet.

Have a friend lay down on the floor. Draw their portrait while sitting above their head so their face is up-side-down. Your drawing will be up-side-down as well.

How would you re-design your hand to be better than it is? If you were into basketball, how might it be different? Consider your hobbies and activities.

What might a flower look like on an alien planet?

Design a new cologne bottle for either a great scent, or something very bad.

Willy Wonka remade an environment out of candy, what would you draw an environment out of?

Create a new label for your favorite beverage.

Pick a playing card and do a design based on that card that no linger looks like a playing card. Use repetition and pattern if it helps.

Create a cover for a ridiculous comic book.

Draw something in the room no one notices.

Lay on the floor and look up. Draw part of the room with this unusual perspective.

Put your leg up on the table and draw your leg, shoe and all, in perspective.

When you cross your eyes, you see double. Draw something around you as if you had double vision. Find a creative way to handle overlapped areas.

Do a portrait of a friend, but re-imagining their hair in a way that shows off their personality.

Draw the trophy you wish you could win.

Draw the first thing you would buy if you won the lottery.

Draw your hand holding your favorite possession.

Draw what it looks like sitting in the front of your car, and put something unexpected in the rear-view mirror.

Draw something pretty next to something ugly.

Draw a piece of popcorn to fill this page.

Draw something floating in a magical way.

Hold a tube of paper up to your eye and draw your point of view. (If you have glasses, maybe you can tape a small tube to them.)

Stand on something tall and draw your view looking down.

While lying on the floor, draw what you see from that perspective as if you were a bug.

Draw an object that makes noise. Draw what you imagine that noise might look like if it could be seen.

Sit in the back of a bus or car and draw your point of view. Feel free to change the scene through the window or make it realistic.

Draw something lit by a candle.

Draw two objects side by side that should never be put together.

Draw two objects side by side that represent opposite themes: War and peace, good and evil, love and hate…

Make a drawing that expresses a lie either literally, figuratively, or symbolically.

Draw an object as if it were in-side-out.

Draw the surface of a coin with a water droplet on it. If you have a magnifying glass, use it.

Draw a soft object with a steel skin with screws, rivets, and bolts.

Draw a cute animal as if it were Frankenstein's pet.

Draw an animal you consider unappealing, as cute.

Draw an object from observation but re-arrange its parts in an unexpected way.

Draw an advertisement for a product you would not like but make it seem appealing.

Draw two objects side by side but change their scale. For example, you might have a giant ant next to a tiny teacup.

Crumple a picture from a magazine and draw it as you see it.

Design a new kind of chair.

Do a line drawing of your shoe, and color it in the way you think would look interesting.

Life is often full of choices. Draw a portrait of yourself, divide the face in half, and show two potential life choices you will need to make as an adult in the design. (You as a teacher or you as a hairdresser) Use symbols and colors in the portrait to show the possible directions your life might take.

Take a common object and draw it as if it was a skeleton. What would the skeleton of a pear look like?

Design a monument for a common object, like a monument to a thumbtack.

Draw a face card from a deck of cards making you the queen, king, jack, or joker.

Draw what you see reflected in a bowl or plate of water. It will reflect better if the bowl is a dark color.

Draw your home or backyard from an aerial perspective. (From above)

Draw a mysterious doorway.

Draw how you would symbolize the 4 seasons.

Design a metal of honor commemorating your greatest achievement in your life so far. If you do not have one you can think of, consider an accomplishment you hope to achieve in the future.

Re-imagine the wrapper for your favorite candy bar. Create a new design for it.

Do a drawing of an object you possess or have nearby, but make it look like its melting.

Draw an object that is reflective. Add a portion of your face into that reflection. (Cell phone, CD, compact, glass of water, spoon, Christmas ball…)

Try to draw an object from 3 points of view but as one object. This is how cubist painters like Picasso and Braque would work.

Find an object and only draw the things around it, leaving the paper white where the object is. We call this negative space drawing.

Scatter a few objects on your table; only draw the parts that overlap.

Draw a landscape with a house, car, or man-made object in it. Give the man-made object natural textures like leaves and grass, and give the natural elements mechanical textures found in the object.

Do a portrait from very careful observation but rearrange the parts of the face.

Create a holiday or birthday card cover in the style of a famous artist.

Do a drawing from observation so lightly that only a person close to the paper can see it.

Draw someone eating, and illustrate behind them, expressive colors, textures, and shapes that you feel would describe the flavor.

Draw the back of someone's head. Try to capture hair without resorting to scribbles.

Draw an eating utensil morphing into something else.

Draw your bedroom as if it was inside a container like a teapot, jar, cardboard box…

Ask the closest person to you pick an object in the area, and then draw it.

Place a few objects on a white piece of paper, only draw the shadows.

Draw what you imagine the inside of your stomach looks like after the last meal you ate.

Imagine you ARE your favorite animal. Do a drawing you think that animal would draw if it could or from its point of view.

Draw a fun pattern for a necktie or bow.

Draw an amazing sand castle on the beach.

Write your initials very large and turn it into a drawing of animals, objects, or other subject.

Draw a new and unique sea creature.

Draw a new and unique dinosaur.

Draw a how-to label or poster for something you know how to do. If it is too complicated, illustrate just 1 to 4 steps of the process.

Draw a simple cartoon that illustrates the last time you were embarrassed.

Draw something with wings that normally would not have them.

Do a drawing of a person combined with an animal. The Egyptians did this a lot.

Create an advertisement for yourself as if you were a product in a store.

Create your initials in a very ornate and decorative way, like old illuminated manuscripts.

Remove your socks and shoes and draw your foot. How would you redesign a common road sign? Yield, Stop, No Running, Poison...

Draw yourself as if you were 100 years old.

Project Reflection:

Title: _____ Media _____

Explanation of the project goals: _____

_____

Description: _____

_____

_____

_____

Connections (To Self, Community, Culture, or traditions) _____

_____

_____

My process: _____

_____

_____

Knowledge I had and applied to this project: _____

_____

_____

Something new I learned or "figured out" through this project: _____

_____

_____

The most successful part of this project was… _____

_____

_____

If I had to do it over again, I would… _____

_____

_____

I hope when others view my work… _____

_____

_____

Project Reflection:

Title: _____ Media _____

Explanation of the project goals: _____
_____

Description:
_____
_____
_____

Connections (To Self, Community, Culture, or traditions) _____
_____
_____

My process: _____
_____
_____

Knowledge I had and applied to this project: _____
_____
_____

Something new I learned or "figured out" through this project: _____
_____
_____

The most successful part of this project was… _____
_____
_____

If I had to do it over again, I would… _____
_____
_____

I hope when others view my work… _____
_____
_____

Project Reflection:

Title: _____ Media _____

Explanation of the project goals: _____

_____

Description:

_____

_____

_____

Connections (To Self, Community, Culture, or traditions) _____

_____

_____

My process: _____

_____

_____

Knowledge I had and applied to this project: _____

_____

_____

Something new I learned or "figured out" through this project: _____

_____

_____

The most successful part of this project was… _____

_____

_____

If I had to do it over again, I would… _____

_____

_____

I hope when others view my work… _____

_____

_____

Project Reflection:

Title: _____ Media _____

Explanation of the project goals: _____

_____

Description:

_____

_____

_____

Connections (To Self, Community, Culture, or traditions) _____

_____

_____

My process: _____

_____

_____

Knowledge I had and applied to this project: _____

_____

_____

Something new I learned or "figured out" through this project: _____

_____

_____

The most successful part of this project was… _____

_____

_____

If I had to do it over again, I would… _____

_____

_____

I hope when others view my work… _____

_____

_____

Project Reflection 2

Title: _____ **Media** _____

Description: (*Describe your work as if you were talking over the phone*)

_____
_____
_____
_____

Describe the main art elements you used. (Line, Shape, Form, Color, Value, Light, Texture.) Write in such a way that it is clear you understand the art elements.

_____
_____
_____
_____

Describe the main art principles you used. (Contrast, Unity, Balance, Emphasis, Variety, Movement, Pattern.) Write in such a way that it is clear you understand the art principles.

_____
_____
_____
_____

(Peer Name) _____ said the most successful part of my project was…

_____
_____
_____

(Peer Name) _____ suggested if I had to do it over again, I should…

_____
_____
_____
_____

Project Reflection 2

Title: _____ Media _____

Description: (*Describe your work as if you were talking over the phone*)

_____
_____
_____
_____
_____

Describe the main art elements you used. (Line, Shape, Form, Color, Value, Light, Texture.) Write in such a way that it is clear you understand the art elements.

_____
_____
_____
_____

Describe the main art principles you used. (Contrast, Unity, Balance, Emphasis, Variety, Movement, Pattern.) Write in such a way that it is clear you understand the art principles.

_____
_____
_____
_____

(Peer Name) _____ said the most successful part of my project was...

_____
_____
_____

(Peer Name) _____ suggested if I had to do it over again, I should...

_____
_____
_____
_____

Project Reflection 2

Title: _____ **Media** _____

Description: (*Describe your work as if you were talking over the phone*)

_____
_____
_____
_____

Describe the main art elements you used. (Line, Shape, Form, Color, Value, Light, Texture.) Write in such a way that it is clear you understand the art elements.

_____
_____
_____
_____

Describe the main art principles you used. (Contrast, Unity, Balance, Emphasis, Variety, Movement, Pattern.) Write in such a way that it is clear you understand the art principles.

_____
_____
_____
_____

(Peer Name) _____ **said the most successful part of my project was…**

_____
_____
_____

(Peer Name) _____ **suggested if I had to do it over again, I should…**

_____
_____
_____

Project Reflection 2

Title: _____ **Media** _____

Description: (*Describe your work as if you were talking over the phone*)

_____
_____
_____
_____

Describe the main art elements you used. (Line, Shape, Form, Color, Value, Light, Texture.) Write in such a way that it is clear you understand the art elements.

_____
_____
_____
_____

Describe the main art principles you used. (Contrast, Unity, Balance, Emphasis, Variety, Movement, Pattern.) Write in such a way that it is clear you understand the art principles.

_____
_____
_____
_____

(Peer Name) _____ **said the most successful part of my project was…**

_____
_____
_____

(Peer Name) _____ **suggested if I had to do it over again, I should…**

_____
_____
_____
_____

Project Reflection 2

Title: _____ **Media** _____

Description: (*Describe your work as if you were talking over the phone*)

_____
_____
_____
_____

Describe the main art elements you used. (Line, Shape, Form, Color, Value, Light, Texture.) Write in such a way that it is clear you understand the art elements.

_____
_____
_____
_____

Describe the main art principles you used. (Contrast, Unity, Balance, Emphasis, Variety, Movement, Pattern.) Write in such a way that it is clear you understand the art principles.

_____
_____
_____
_____

(Peer Name) _____ **said the most successful part of my project was…**

_____
_____
_____

(Peer Name) _____ **suggested if I had to do it over again, I should…**

_____
_____
_____
_____

The best thing about the artwork is:

The work could be improved by:

Another good thing about the artwork is:

The best thing about the artwork is:

The work could be improved by:

Another good thing about the artwork is:

Formal Critique:

Title _____ Artist _____ Year _____

Describe the art as if you are explaining it over the phone.

_____

_____

_____

Check what you included: [_] Media, [_] Elements, [_] Style/Genre, [_] Objects, [_] Technique

Analysis: Describe how the artist used the art principles.
(Unity, Contrast, Balance, Emphasis, Variety, Movement, Pattern)

_____

_____

_____

_____

Interpretation: Use evidence from above to explain the meaning or message of the work.

_____

_____

_____

_____

Evaluation: Judge the work explaining why you feel that way. (Is there room for improvement?)

_____

_____

_____

_____

Formal Critique:

Title _____ Artist _____ Year _____

Describe the art as if you are explaining it over the phone.

_____

_____

_____

_____

Check what you included: [_] Media, [_] Elements, [_] Style/Genre, [_] Objects, [_] Technique

Analysis: Describe how the artist used the art principles.
(Unity, Contrast, Balance, Emphasis, Variety, Movement, Pattern)

_____

_____

_____

_____

Interpretation: Use evidence from above to explain the meaning or message of the work.

_____

_____

_____

_____

Evaluation: Judge the work explaining why you feel that way. (Is there room for improvement?)

_____

_____

_____

_____

Formal Critique:

Title _____ Artist _____ Year _____

Describe the art as if you are explaining it over the phone.

_____

_____

_____

_____

Check what you included: [_] Media, [_] Elements, [_] Style/Genre, [_] Objects, [_] Technique

Analysis: Describe how the artist used the art principles.
(Unity, Contrast, Balance, Emphasis, Variety, Movement, Pattern)

_____

_____

_____

_____

Interpretation: Use evidence from above to explain the meaning or message of the work.

_____

_____

_____

_____

Evaluation: Judge the work explaining why you feel that way. (Is there room for improvement?)

_____

_____

_____

_____

Formal Critique:

Title _____ Artist _____ Year _____

Describe the art as if you are explaining it over the phone.

_____

_____

_____

_____

Check what you included: [_] Media, [_] Elements, [_] Style/Genre, [_] Objects, [_] Technique

Analysis: Describe how the artist used the art principles.
(Unity, Contrast, Balance, Emphasis, Variety, Movement, Pattern)

_____

_____

_____

_____

Interpretation: Use evidence from above to explain the meaning or message of the work.

_____

_____

_____

_____

Evaluation: Judge the work explaining why you feel that way. (Is there room for improvement?)

_____

_____

_____

_____

End of Class Survey

1. What was your favorite project of the year/semester and why?

_____

_____

2. What was your least favorite project of the year/semester and why?

_____

_____

3. Did you feel the teacher was able to allow you enough freedom to express your own "artistic voice?" Please give an example of your experience here.

_____

_____

4. What was something you learned that you feel you will remember most?

_____

_____

5. What is the most positive thing you can say about having art class?

_____

_____

6. What advice would you give your teacher to consider for next year?

_____

_____

7. Anything else you might like to say or share?

_____

_____

Draw the person sitting next to you on the next page and compare this to your first drawing.

Who did you draw? _____

Compare this drawing with the one you did in the beginning of this workbook

Assessing your work:

We do not grade work based on how "pretty" it is. You are assessed on five points. 1. You are usually given some requirements or targets to meet (or exceed.) 2. You will be expected to document your project through sketches, peer critiques, research, notes, and other artifacts. 3. You are expected to be on-task and to complete your work on or close to schedule. 4. As you work, you are expected to use supplies thoughtfully, ensuring there is no waste and care for your artwork by not shoving it into a bookbag, or letting your dog chew on it. 5. In most cases, you will need to incorporate yourself, opinions, culture, point of view, interests, experiences, etc. into your work to make it uniquely yours.

When you meet expectations, you can earn your "A" grade, or 90%. To get a higher grade, you need to push yourself to exceed expectations in one or more of these 5 areas.

	Criteria					Points
	100% / 20pts Exceeds Expectations	90% / 18pts Meets Expectations	80% / 16pts Approaches Exp.	70% - 65% / 14pts Missed Exp.	0/F	
Project Requirements	I exceeded expectations by:	Expected use & combination of art elements & principles. Work included all requirements.	Acceptable use of art elements & principles but lacked depth in exploring requirements.	Lacks evidence of thoughtful use of elements & principles with a design that looks unplanned, rushed, &/or incomplete.		____
Process, Research & Documentation	I exceeded expectations by:	Research and documentation are present and meet expectations. Writing and sketches are complete and purposeful.	Research and/or documentation is present but thin. Artist did not fully take advantage of pre-work opportunities.	Research and/or documentation was missing & had a negative impact on the final work. Evidence of depth was lacking.		____
Time & Management	I exceeded expectations by:	Student was mostly independently motivated with a few social distractions. Work was mostly self-driven.	Student was somewhat distracted from their work OR finished early without using the extra time to push the depth or quality.	Often reminded to stay on task. Social/digital interactions impeded work. Lack of focus had a strong impact on project work.		____
Detail, Complexity, Craftsmanship, & Care	I exceeded expectations by:	Materials & techniques were explored & met project expectations. Many visual challenges were attempted. Midia is without folds/rips or evidence of poor handling.	Media or technique was not fully explored. Visual challenges were minimal. Media handling could have avoided minor rips or folds.	Media & techniques show little evidence of exploration. Visual challenges were avoided. Evidence of poor handling or storage may have an impact as well.		____
Original, Personal, & Unique (Always credit your inspirations)	100% original & highly personal because:	Generally personal & unique but inspired by:	Topically personalized and based on:	Topical and highly derivative of:	Copied	

Project Progress Document   Name _____ pd ____

This paper will document your daily participation, progress, feedback, & grade.

Project Title: _____

My reference or inspirations for this project is: _____

My personal connection: _____

_____

Intro. date   ___/___/_____

DEADLINE: ___/___/_____

Requirements:

1. _____

2. _____

3. _____

To exceed expectations, I can...

1. _____

2. _____

3. _____

Peer Feedback by _____

Actionable advice for success: _____

_____

_____

...Instructor Section Only...	
10% _____	Sketch
20% _____	
25% _____ (quarter)	
30% _____	Project Work Phase
40% _____	
50% _____ (half)	
60% _____	
70% _____	
75% _____ (3/4)	
80% _____	Detail & finishing
85% _____	
90% _____	
95% _____	
(Percent complete, not a grade)	

_____

_____

_____

I will take this advice: [__] Yes or [__] No thank you.

Name _____ Title _____ Pd._____

Universal Art Project Rubric

	Criteria					Points
	100% / 20pts Exceeds Expectations	90% / 18pts Meets Expectations	80% / 16pts Approaches Exp.	70% - 65% / 14pts Missed Exp.	0/F	
Project Requirements	I exceeded expectations by:	Expected use & combination of art elements & principles. Work included all requirements.	Acceptable use of art elements & principles but lacked depth in exploring requirements.	Lacks evidence of thoughtful use of elements & principles & minimally met required components.		____
Process, Research & Documentation	I exceeded expectations by:	Research & documentation are present & meet expectations. Prewriting & sketches are complete & purposeful.	Research and/or documentation is present but thin. Artist did not fully take advantage of pre-work opportunities.	Research and/or documentation was missing & had a negative impact on the final work. Evidence of depth was lacking.		____
Time & Management	I exceeded expectations by:	Student was mostly independently motivated with a few social and/or digital distractions. Work was mostly self-driven.	Student was sometimes distracted from work **OR** finished early without using the extra time to exceed expectations or stay active in art-making.	Often reminded to stay on task. Social/digital interactions impeded work. Lack of focus had a strong impact on project work.		____
Detail, Complexity, Craftsmanship, & Care	I exceeded expectations by:	Media is without folds/rips or evidence of poor handling. Materials & techniques were explored & met handling expectations. Visual challenges were attempted.	Media handling could have avoided minor rips or folds. Media or technique was not fully explored. Visual challenges were minimal.	Poor handling or storage had an impact. Media & techniques show little evidence of exploration. Visual challenges were avoided.		____
Original, Personal, & Unique (Always credit your inspirations)	100% original & highly personal because:	Generally personal & unique but inspired by:	Topically personalized & based on:	Topical & highly derivative of:	Copied	

Comments:

Grade ____

Created by www.artedguru.com & www.FirehousePublications.com

If you could do this project again, what might you do differently?

Project Progress Document   Name _____ pd ____

This paper will document your daily participation, progress, feedback, & grade.

Project Title: _____

My reference or inspirations for this project is: _____

My personal connection: _____

_____

Intro. date   ___/___/_____

DEADLINE: ___/___/_____

Requirements:

1. _____

2. _____

3. _____

To exceed expectations, I can…

1. _____

2. _____

3. _____

Peer Feedback by _____

Actionable advice for success: _____

_____

_____

...Instructor Section Only...	
10% _____	Sketch
20% _____	
25% _____ (quarter)	
30 % _____	Project Work Phase
40% _____	
50% _____ (half)	
60% _____	
70% _____	
75% _____ (3/4)	
80% _____	Detail & finishing
85% _____	
90% _____	
95% _____	
(Percent complete, not a grade)	

_____

_____

_____

I will take this advice: [__] Yes or [__] No thank you.

Name _____ Title _____ Pd. _____

Universal Art Project Rubric

	Criteria				Points
	100% / 20pts Exceeds Expectations	90% / 18pts Meets Expectations	80% / 16pts Approaches Exp.	70% - 65% / 14pts Missed Exp.	0/F
Project Requirements	*I exceeded expectations by:*	Expected use & combination of art elements & principles. Work included all requirements.	Acceptable use of art elements & principles but lacked depth in exploring requirements.	Lacks evidence of thoughtful use of elements & principles & minimally met required components.	_____
Process, Research & Documentation	*I exceeded expectations by:*	Research & documentation are present & meet expectations. Prewriting & sketches are complete & purposeful.	Research and/or documentation is present but thin. Artist did not fully take advantage of pre-work opportunities.	Research and/or documentation was missing & had a negative impact on the final work. Evidence of depth was lacking.	_____
Time & Management	*I exceeded expectations by:*	Student was mostly independently motivated with a few social and/or digital distractions. Work was mostly self-driven.	Student was sometimes distracted from work **OR** finished early without using the extra time to exceed expectations or stay active in art-making.	Often reminded to stay on task. Social/digital interactions impeded work. Lack of focus had a strong impact on project work.	_____
Detail, Complexity, Craftsmanship, & Care	*I exceeded expectations by:*	Media is without folds/rips or evidence of poor handling. Materials & techniques were explored & met handling expectations. Visual challenges were attempted.	Media handling could have avoided minor rips or folds. Media or technique was not fully explored. Visual challenges were minimal.	Poor handling or storage had an impact. Media & techniques show little evidence of exploration. Visual challenges were avoided.	_____
Original, Personal, & Unique **(Always credit your inspirations)**	100% original & highly personal because:	Generally personal & unique but inspired by:	Topically personalized & based on:	Topical & highly derivative of:	Copied
Comments:					**Grade** _____

Created by www.artedguru.com & www.FirehousePublications.com

If you could do this project again, what might you do differently?

Project Progress Document

Name _____ pd ____

This paper will document your daily participation, progress, feedback, & grade.

Project Title: _____

My reference or inspirations for this project is: _____

My personal connection: _____

_____

Intro. date ___/___/_____

DEADLINE: ___/___/_____

Requirements:

1. _____

2. _____

3. _____

To exceed expectations, I can…

1. _____

2. _____

3. _____

Peer Feedback by _____

Actionable advice for success: _____

_____

_____

...Instructor Section Only...

10% _____   *Sketch*

20% _____

25% _____ (quarter)

30% _____   *Project Work Phase*

40% _____

50% _____ (half)

60% _____

70% _____

75% _____ (3/4)

80% _____   *Detail & finishing*

85% _____

90% _____

95% _____

(Percent complete, not a grade)

I will take this advice: [__] Yes or [__] No thank you.

Name _____ Title _____ Pd._____

Universal Art Project Rubric

	Criteria					Points
	100% / 20pts Exceeds Expectations	90% / 18pts Meets Expectations	80% / 16pts Approaches Exp.	70% - 65% / 14pts Missed Exp.	0/F	
Project Requirements	I exceeded expectations by:	Expected use & combination of art elements & principles. Work included all requirements.	Acceptable use of art elements & principles but lacked depth in exploring requirements.	Lacks evidence of thoughtful use of elements & principles & minimally met required components.		____
Process, Research & Documentation	I exceeded expectations by:	Research & documentation are present & meet expectations. Prewriting & sketches are complete & purposeful.	Research and/or documentation is present but thin. Artist did not fully take advantage of pre-work opportunities.	Research and/or documentation was missing & had a negative impact on the final work. Evidence of depth was lacking.		____
Time & Management	I exceeded expectations by:	Student was mostly independently motivated with a few social and/or digital distractions. Work was mostly self-driven.	Student was sometimes distracted from work **OR** finished early without using the extra time to exceed expectations or stay active in art-making.	Often reminded to stay on task. Social/digital interactions impeded work. Lack of focus had a strong impact on project work.		____
Detail, Complexity, Craftsmanship, & Care	I exceeded expectations by:	Media is without folds/rips or evidence of poor handling. Materials & techniques were explored & met handling expectations. Visual challenges were attempted.	Media handling could have avoided minor rips or folds. Media or technique was not fully explored. Visual challenges were minimal.	Poor handling or storage had an impact. Media & techniques show little evidence of exploration. Visual challenges were avoided.		____
Original, Personal, & Unique (Always credit your inspirations)	100% original & highly personal because:	Generally personal & unique but inspired by:	Topically personalized & based on:	Topical & highly derivative of:	Copied	

Comments:

Grade ____

Created by www.artedguru.com & www.FirehousePublications.com

If you could do this project again, what might you do differently?

Project Progress Document Name _____ pd ____

This paper will document your daily participation, progress, feedback, & grade.

Project Title: _____

My reference or inspirations for this project is: _____

My personal connection: _____

_____

Intro. date ___/___/_____

DEADLINE: ___/___/_____

Requirements:

1. _____
2. _____
3. _____

To exceed expectations, I can…

1. _____
2. _____
3. _____

Peer Feedback by _____

Actionable advice for success: _____

_____

_____

_____

_____

I will take this advice: [__] Yes or [__] No thank you.

…Instructor Section Only…

10% _____	Sketch
20% _____	
25% _____ (quarter)	
30% _____	Project Work Phase
40% _____	
50% _____ (half)	
60% _____	
70% _____	
75% _____ (3/4)	
80% _____	Detail & finishing
85% _____	
90% _____	
95% _____	

(Percent complete, not a grade)

Name _____ Title _____ Pd._____

Universal Art Project Rubric

	Criteria				Points
	100% / 20pts Exceeds Expectations	90% / 18pts Meets Expectations	80% / 16pts Approaches Exp.	70% - 65% / 14pts Missed Exp.	0/F
Project Requirements	*I exceeded expectations by:*	Expected use & combination of art elements & principles. Work included all requirements.	Acceptable use of art elements & principles but lacked depth in exploring requirements.	Lacks evidence of thoughtful use of elements & principles & minimally met required components.	____
Process, Research & Documentation	*I exceeded expectations by:*	Research & documentation are present & meet expectations. Prewriting & sketches are complete & purposeful.	Research and/or documentation is present but thin. Artist did not fully take advantage of pre-work opportunities.	Research and/or documentation was missing & had a negative impact on the final work. Evidence of depth was lacking.	____
Time & Management	*I exceeded expectations by:*	Student was mostly independently motivated with a few social and/or digital distractions. Work was mostly self-driven.	Student was sometimes distracted from work **OR** finished early without using the extra time to exceed expectations or stay active in art-making.	Often reminded to stay on task. Social/digital interactions impeded work. Lack of focus had a strong impact on project work.	____
Detail, Complexity, Craftsmanship, & Care	*I exceeded expectations by:*	Media is without folds/rips or evidence of poor handling. Materials & techniques were explored & met handling expectations. Visual challenges were attempted.	Media handling could have avoided minor rips or folds. Media or technique was not fully explored. Visual challenges were minimal.	Poor handling or storage had an impact. Media & techniques show little evidence of exploration. Visual challenges were avoided.	____
Original, Personal, & Unique (Always credit your inspirations)	100% original & highly personal because:	Generally personal & unique but inspired by:	Topically personalized & based on:	Topical & highly derivative of:	Copied
Comments:					**Grade** ____

Created by www.artedguru.com & www.FirehousePublications.com

If you could do this project again, what might you do differently?

Project Progress Document   Name _____ pd ____

This paper will document your daily participation, progress, feedback, & grade.

Project Title: _____

My reference or inspirations for this project is: _____

My personal connection: _____

_____

Intro. date   ___/___/_____

DEADLINE: ___/___/_____

Requirements:

1. _____

2. _____

3. _____

To exceed expectations, I can…

1. _____

2. _____

3. _____

Peer Feedback by _____

Actionable advice for success: _____

_____

...Instructor Section Only...	
10% _____	Sketch
20% _____	
25% _____ (quarter)	
30% _____	Project Work Phase
40% _____	
50% _____ (half)	
60% _____	
70% _____	
75% _____ (3/4)	
80% _____	Detail & finishing
85% _____	
90% _____	
95% _____	
(Percent complete, not a grade)	

_____

_____

I will take this advice: [__] Yes or [__] No thank you.

Name _____ Title _____ Pd. _____

Universal Art Project Rubric

	Criteria					Points
	100% / 20pts Exceeds Expectations	90% / 18pts Meets Expectations	80% / 16pts Approaches Exp.	70% - 65% / 14pts Missed Exp.	0/F	
Project Requirements	I exceeded expectations by:	Expected use & combination of art elements & principles. Work included all requirements.	Acceptable use of art elements & principles but lacked depth in exploring requirements.	Lacks evidence of thoughtful use of elements & principles & minimally met required components.		____
Process, Research & Documentation	I exceeded expectations by:	Research & documentation are present & meet expectations. Prewriting & sketches are complete & purposeful.	Research and/or documentation is present but thin. Artist did not fully take advantage of pre-work opportunities.	Research and/or documentation was missing & had a negative impact on the final work. Evidence of depth was lacking.		____
Time & Management	I exceeded expectations by:	Student was mostly independently motivated with a few social and/or digital distractions. Work was mostly self-driven.	Student was sometimes distracted from work **OR** finished early without using the extra time to exceed expectations or stay active in art-making.	Often reminded to stay on task. Social/digital interactions impeded work. Lack of focus had a strong impact on project work.		____
Detail, Complexity, Craftsmanship, & Care	I exceeded expectations by:	Media is without folds/rips or evidence of poor handling. Materials & techniques were explored & met handling expectations. Visual challenges were attempted.	Media handling could have avoided minor rips or folds. Media or technique was not fully explored. Visual challenges were minimal.	Poor handling or storage had an impact. Media & techniques show little evidence of exploration. Visual challenges were avoided.		____
Original, Personal, & Unique (Always credit your inspirations)	100% original & highly personal because:	Generally personal & unique but inspired by:	Topically personalized & based on:	Topical & highly derivative of:	Copied	

Comments:

Grade ____

Created by www.artedguru.com & www.FirehousePublications.com

If you could do this project again, what might you do differently?

Project Progress Document   Name _____ pd ____

This paper will document your daily participation, progress, feedback, & grade.

Project Title: _____

My reference or inspirations for this project is: _____

My personal connection: _____

_____

Intro. date   ___/___/_____

DEADLINE: ___/___/_____

Requirements:

1. _____

2. _____

3. _____

To exceed expectations, I can…

1. _____

2. _____

3. _____

Peer Feedback by _____

Actionable advice for success: _____

_____

...Instructor Section Only...

10% _____   *Sketch*

20% _____

25% _____ (quarter)

30 % _____   *Project Work Phase*

40% _____

50% _____ (half)

60% _____

70% _____

75% _____ (3/4)

80% _____   *Detail & finishing*

85% _____

90% _____

95% _____

(Percent complete, not a grade)

_____

_____

_____

I will take this advice: [__] Yes or [__] No thank you.

Name _____ Title _____ Pd._____

Universal Art Project Rubric

	Criteria					Points
	100% / 20pts Exceeds Expectations	90% / 18pts Meets Expectations	80% / 16pts Approaches Exp.	70% - 65% / 14pts Missed Exp.	0/F	
Project Requirements	I exceeded expectations by:	Expected use & combination of art elements & principles. Work included all requirements.	Acceptable use of art elements & principles but lacked depth in exploring requirements.	Lacks evidence of thoughtful use of elements & principles & minimally met required components.		____
Process, Research & Documentation	I exceeded expectations by:	Research & documentation are present & meet expectations. Prewriting & sketches are complete & purposeful.	Research and/or documentation is present but thin. Artist did not fully take advantage of pre-work opportunities.	Research and/or documentation was missing & had a negative impact on the final work. Evidence of depth was lacking.		____
Time & Management	I exceeded expectations by:	Student was mostly independently motivated with a few social and/or digital distractions. Work was mostly self-driven.	Student was sometimes distracted from work **OR** finished early without using the extra time to exceed expectations or stay active in art-making.	Often reminded to stay on task. Social/digital interactions impeded work. Lack of focus had a strong impact on project work.		____
Detail, Complexity, Craftsmanship, & Care	I exceeded expectations by:	Media is without folds/rips or evidence of poor handling. Materials & techniques were explored & met handling expectations. Visual challenges were attempted.	Media handling could have avoided minor rips or folds. Media or technique was not fully explored. Visual challenges were minimal.	Poor handling or storage had an impact. Media & techniques show little evidence of exploration. Visual challenges were avoided.		____
Original, Personal, & Unique (Always credit your inspirations)	100% original & highly personal because:	Generally personal & unique but inspired by:	Topically personalized & based on:	Topical & highly derivative of:	Copied	
Comments:					**Grade** ____

Created by www.artedguru.com & www.FirehousePublications.com

If you could do this project again, what might you do differently?

Project Progress Document   Name _____ pd ____

This paper will document your daily participation, progress, feedback, & grade.

Project Title: _____

My reference or inspirations for this project is: _____

My personal connection: _____

_____

Intro. date   ___/___/_____

DEADLINE: ___/___/_____

Requirements:

1. _____

2. _____

3. _____

To exceed expectations, I can…

1. _____

2. _____

3. _____

Peer Feedback by _____

Actionable advice for success: _____

_____

...Instructor Section Only...	
10% _____	Sketch
20% _____	
25% _____ (quarter)	
30 % _____	Project Work Phase
40% _____	
50% _____ (half)	
60% _____	
70% _____	
75% _____ (3/4)	
80% _____	Detail & finishing
85% _____	
90% _____	
95% _____	
(Percent complete, not a grade)	

_____

_____

_____

I will take this advice: [__] Yes or [__] No thank you.

Name _____ Title _____ Pd. _____

Universal Art Project Rubric

	Criteria					Points
	100% / 20pts Exceeds Expectations	90% / 18pts Meets Expectations	80% / 16pts Approaches Exp.	70% - 65% / 14pts Missed Exp.	0/F	
Project Requirements	I exceeded expectations by:	Expected use & combination of art elements & principles. Work included all requirements.	Acceptable use of art elements & principles but lacked depth in exploring requirements.	Lacks evidence of thoughtful use of elements & principles & minimally met required components.		____
Process, Research & Documentation	I exceeded expectations by:	Research & documentation are present & meet expectations. Prewriting & sketches are complete & purposeful.	Research and/or documentation is present but thin. Artist did not fully take advantage of pre-work opportunities.	Research and/or documentation was missing & had a negative impact on the final work. Evidence of depth was lacking.		____
Time & Management	I exceeded expectations by:	Student was mostly independently motivated with a few social and/or digital distractions. Work was mostly self-driven.	Student was sometimes distracted from work **OR** finished early without using the extra time to exceed expectations or stay active in art-making.	Often reminded to stay on task. Social/digital interactions impeded work. Lack of focus had a strong impact on project work.		____
Detail, Complexity, Craftsmanship, & Care	I exceeded expectations by:	Media is without folds/rips or evidence of poor handling. Materials & techniques were explored & met handling expectations. Visual challenges were attempted.	Media handling could have avoided minor rips or folds. Media or technique was not fully explored. Visual challenges were minimal.	Poor handling or storage had an impact. Media & techniques show little evidence of exploration. Visual challenges were avoided.		____
Original, Personal, & Unique (Always credit your inspirations)	100% original & highly personal because:	Generally personal & unique but inspired by:	Topically personalized & based on:	Topical & highly derivative of:	Copied	
Comments:						Grade ____

Created by www.artedguru.com & www.FirehousePublications.com

If you could do this project again, what might you do differently?

Project Progress Document   Name _____ pd ____

This paper will document your daily participation, progress, feedback, & grade.

Project Title: _____

My reference or inspirations for this project is: _____

My personal connection: _____

_____

Intro. date   ___/___/_____

DEADLINE: ___/___/_____

Requirements:

1. _____

2. _____

3. _____

To exceed expectations, I can…

1. _____

2. _____

3. _____

Peer Feedback by _____

Actionable advice for success: _____

_____

...Instructor Section Only...	
10% _____	Sketch
20% _____	
25% _____ (quarter)	
30 % _____	Project Work Phase
40% _____	
50% _____ (half)	
60% _____	
70% _____	
75% _____ (3/4)	
80% _____	Detail & finishing
85% _____	
90% _____	
95% _____	
(Percent complete, not a grade)	

_____

_____

_____

I will take this advice: [__] Yes or [__] No thank you.

Name _____ Title _____ Pd. _____

Universal Art Project Rubric

	Criteria				Points
	100% / 20pts Exceeds Expectations	90% / 18pts Meets Expectations	80% / 16pts Approaches Exp.	70% - 65% / 14pts Missed Exp.	0/F
Project Requirements	*I exceeded expectations by:*	Expected use & combination of art elements & principles. Work included all requirements.	Acceptable use of art elements & principles but lacked depth in exploring requirements.	Lacks evidence of thoughtful use of elements & principles & minimally met required components.	____
Process, Research & Documentation	*I exceeded expectations by:*	Research & documentation are present & meet expectations. Prewriting & sketches are complete & purposeful.	Research and/or documentation is present but thin. Artist did not fully take advantage of pre-work opportunities.	Research and/or documentation was missing & had a negative impact on the final work. Evidence of depth was lacking.	____
Time & Management	*I exceeded expectations by:*	Student was mostly independently motivated with a few social and/or digital distractions. Work was mostly self-driven.	Student was sometimes distracted from work **OR** finished early without using the extra time to exceed expectations or stay active in art-making.	Often reminded to stay on task. Social/digital interactions impeded work. Lack of focus had a strong impact on project work.	____
Detail, Complexity, Craftsmanship, & Care	*I exceeded expectations by:*	Media is without folds/rips or evidence of poor handling. Materials & techniques were explored & met handling expectations. Visual challenges were attempted.	Media handling could have avoided minor rips or folds. Media or technique was not fully explored. Visual challenges were minimal.	Poor handling or storage had an impact. Media & techniques show little evidence of exploration. Visual challenges were avoided.	____
Original, Personal, & Unique (Always credit your inspirations)	100% original & highly personal because:	Generally personal & unique but inspired by:	Topically personalized & based on:	Topical & highly derivative of:	Copied

Comments:

Grade ____

Created by www.artedguru.com & www.FirehousePublications.com

If you could do this project again, what might you do differently?

Project Progress Document   Name _____ pd ____

This paper will document your daily participation, progress, feedback, & grade.

Project Title: _____

My reference or inspirations for this project is: _____

My personal connection: _____

_____

Intro. date   ___/___/_____

DEADLINE: ___/___/_____

Requirements:

1. _____

2. _____

3. _____

To exceed expectations, I can…

1. _____

2. _____

3. _____

Peer Feedback by _____

Actionable advice for success: _____

_____

…Instructor Section Only…

10% _____ | Sketch

20% _____

25% _____ (quarter)

30 % _____ | Project Work Phase

40% _____

50% _____ (half)

60% _____

70% _____

75% _____ (3/4)

80% _____ | Detail & finishing

85% _____

90% _____

95% _____

(Percent complete, not a grade)

_____

_____

_____

I will take this advice: [__] Yes or [__] No thank you.

Name _____ Title _____ Pd. _____

Universal Art Project Rubric

	Criteria					Points
	100% / 20pts Exceeds Expectations	90% / 18pts Meets Expectations	80% / 16pts Approaches Exp.	70% - 65% / 14pts Missed Exp.	0/F	
Project Requirements	*I exceeded expectations by:*	Expected use & combination of art elements & principles. Work included all requirements.	Acceptable use of art elements & principles but lacked depth in exploring requirements.	Lacks evidence of thoughtful use of elements & principles & minimally met required components.		____
Process, Research & Documentation	*I exceeded expectations by:*	Research & documentation are present & meet expectations. Prewriting & sketches are complete & purposeful.	Research and/or documentation is present but thin. Artist did not fully take advantage of pre-work opportunities.	Research and/or documentation was missing & had a negative impact on the final work. Evidence of depth was lacking.		____
Time & Management	*I exceeded expectations by:*	Student was mostly independently motivated with a few social and/or digital distractions. Work was mostly self-driven.	Student was sometimes distracted from work **OR** finished early without using the extra time to exceed expectations or stay active in art-making.	Often reminded to stay on task. Social/digital interactions impeded work. Lack of focus had a strong impact on project work.		____
Detail, Complexity, Craftsmanship, & Care	*I exceeded expectations by:*	Media is without folds/rips or evidence of poor handling. Materials & techniques were explored & met handling expectations. Visual challenges were attempted.	Media handling could have avoided minor rips or folds. Media or technique was not fully explored. Visual challenges were minimal.	Poor handling or storage had an impact. Media & techniques show little evidence of exploration. Visual challenges were avoided.		____
Original, Personal, & Unique (Always credit your inspirations)	100% original & highly personal because:	Generally personal & unique but inspired by:	Topically personalized & based on:	Topical & highly derivative of:	Copied	
Comments:					**Grade** ____	

Created by www.artedguru.com & www.FirehousePublications.com

If you could do this project again, what might you do differently?

Project Progress Document   Name _____ pd ____

This paper will document your daily participation, progress, feedback, & grade.

Project Title: _____

My reference or inspirations for this project is: _____

My personal connection: _____

_____

Intro. date ___/___/_____

DEADLINE: ___/___/_____

Requirements:

1. _____

2. _____

3. _____

To exceed expectations, I can…

1. _____

2. _____

3. _____

Peer Feedback by _____

Actionable advice for success: _____

_____

_____

_____

...Instructor Section Only...	
10% _____	Sketch
20% _____	
25% _____ (quarter)	
30% _____	Project Work Phase
40% _____	
50% _____ (half)	
60% _____	
70% _____	
75% _____ (3/4)	
80% _____	Detail & finishing
85% _____	
90% _____	
95% _____	
(Percent complete, not a grade)	

I will take this advice: [__] Yes or [__] No thank you.

Name _____ Title _____ Pd. _____

Universal Art Project Rubric

	Criteria					Points
	100% / 20pts Exceeds Expectations	90% / 18pts Meets Expectations	80% / 16pts Approaches Exp.	70% - 65% / 14pts Missed Exp.	0/F	
Project Requirements	I exceeded expectations by:	Expected use & combination of art elements & principles. Work included all requirements.	Acceptable use of art elements & principles but lacked depth in exploring requirements.	Lacks evidence of thoughtful use of elements & principles & minimally met required components.		____
Process, Research & Documentation	I exceeded expectations by:	Research & documentation are present & meet expectations. Prewriting & sketches are complete & purposeful.	Research and/or documentation is present but thin. Artist did not fully take advantage of pre-work opportunities.	Research and/or documentation was missing & had a negative impact on the final work. Evidence of depth was lacking.		____
Time & Management	I exceeded expectations by:	Student was mostly independently motivated with a few social and/or digital distractions. Work was mostly self-driven.	Student was sometimes distracted from work **OR** finished early without using the extra time to exceed expectations or stay active in art-making.	Often reminded to stay on task. Social/digital interactions impeded work. Lack of focus had a strong impact on project work.		____
Detail, Complexity, Craftsmanship, & Care	I exceeded expectations by:	Media is without folds/rips or evidence of poor handling. Materials & techniques were explored & met handling expectations. Visual challenges were attempted.	Media handling could have avoided minor rips or folds. Media or technique was not fully explored. Visual challenges were minimal.	Poor handling or storage had an impact. Media & techniques show little evidence of exploration. Visual challenges were avoided.		____
Original, Personal, & Unique (Always credit your inspirations)	100% original & highly personal because:	Generally personal & unique but inspired by:	Topically personalized & based on:	Topical & highly derivative of:	Copied	
Comments:						**Grade** ____

Created by www.artedguru.com & www.FirehousePublications.com

If you could do this project again, what might you do differently?

Project Progress Document Name _____ pd ____

This paper will document your daily participation, progress, feedback, & grade.

Project Title: _____

My reference or inspirations for this project is: _____

My personal connection: _____

_____

Intro. date ___/___/_____

DEADLINE: ___/___/_____

Requirements:

1. _____

2. _____

3. _____

To exceed expectations, I can...

1. _____

2. _____

3. _____

Peer Feedback by _____

Actionable advice for success: _____

_____

_____

...Instructor Section Only...	
10% _____	Sketch
20% _____	
25% _____ (quarter)	
30% _____	Project Work Phase
40% _____	
50% _____ (half)	
60% _____	
70% _____	
75% _____ (3/4)	
80% _____	Detail & finishing
85% _____	
90% _____	
95% _____	
(Percent complete, not a grade)	

_____

_____

I will take this advice: [__] Yes or [__] No thank you.

Name _____ Title _____ Pd. _____

Universal Art Project Rubric

	Criteria					Points
	100% / 20pts Exceeds Expectations	90% / 18pts Meets Expectations	80% / 16pts Approaches Exp.	70% - 65% / 14pts Missed Exp.	0/F	
Project Requirements	I exceeded expectations by:	Expected use & combination of art elements & principles. Work included all requirements.	Acceptable use of art elements & principles but lacked depth in exploring requirements.	Lacks evidence of thoughtful use of elements & principles & minimally met required components.		___
Process, Research & Documentation	I exceeded expectations by:	Research & documentation are present & meet expectations. Prewriting & sketches are complete & purposeful.	Research and/or documentation is present but thin. Artist did not fully take advantage of pre-work opportunities.	Research and/or documentation was missing & had a negative impact on the final work. Evidence of depth was lacking.		___
Time & Management	I exceeded expectations by:	Student was mostly independently motivated with a few social and/or digital distractions. Work was mostly self-driven.	Student was sometimes distracted from work **OR** finished early without using the extra time to exceed expectations or stay active in art-making.	Often reminded to stay on task. Social/digital interactions impeded work. Lack of focus had a strong impact on project work.		___
Detail, Complexity, Craftsmanship, & Care	I exceeded expectations by:	Media is without folds/rips or evidence of poor handling. Materials & techniques were explored & met handling expectations. Visual challenges were attempted.	Media handling could have avoided minor rips or folds. Media or technique was not fully explored. Visual challenges were minimal.	Poor handling or storage had an impact. Media & techniques show little evidence of exploration. Visual challenges were avoided.		___
Original, Personal, & Unique (Always credit your inspirations)	100% original & highly personal because:	Generally personal & unique but inspired by:	Topically personalized & based on:	Topical & highly derivative of:	Copied	
Comments:					**Grade** ___	

Created by www.artedguru.com & www.FirehousePublications.com

If you could do this project again, what might you do differently?

Project Progress Document   Name _____ pd ____

This paper will document your daily participation, progress, feedback, & grade.

Project Title: _____

My reference or inspirations for this project is: _____

My personal connection: _____

_____

Intro. date ___/___/_____

DEADLINE: ___/___/_____

Requirements:

1. _____

2. _____

3. _____

To exceed expectations, I can…

1. _____

2. _____

3. _____

Peer Feedback by _____

Actionable advice for success: _____

_____

_____

...Instructor Section Only...	
10% _____	Sketch
20% _____	
25% _____ (quarter)	
30 % _____	Project Work Phase
40% _____	
50% _____ (half)	
60% _____	
70% _____	
75% _____ (3/4)	
80% _____	Detail & finishing
85% _____	
90% _____	
95% _____	
(Percent complete, not a grade)	

_____

I will take this advice: [__] Yes or [__] No thank you.

Name _____ Title _____ Pd._____

Universal Art Project Rubric

	Criteria				Points
	100% / 20pts Exceeds Expectations	90% / 18pts Meets Expectations	80% / 16pts Approaches Exp.	70% - 65% / 14pts Missed Exp.	0/F
Project Requirements	I exceeded expectations by:	Expected use & combination of art elements & principles. Work included all requirements.	Acceptable use of art elements & principles but lacked depth in exploring requirements.	Lacks evidence of thoughtful use of elements & principles & minimally met required components.	____
Process, Research & Documentation	I exceeded expectations by:	Research & documentation are present & meet expectations. Prewriting & sketches are complete & purposeful.	Research and/or documentation is present but thin. Artist did not fully take advantage of pre-work opportunities.	Research and/or documentation was missing & had a negative impact on the final work. Evidence of depth was lacking.	____
Time & Management	I exceeded expectations by:	Student was mostly independently motivated with a few social and/or digital distractions. Work was mostly self-driven.	Student was sometimes distracted from work OR finished early without using the extra time to exceed expectations or stay active in art-making.	Often reminded to stay on task. Social/digital interactions impeded work. Lack of focus had a strong impact on project work.	____
Detail, Complexity, Craftsmanship, & Care	I exceeded expectations by:	Media is without folds/rips or evidence of poor handling. Materials & techniques were explored & met handling expectations. Visual challenges were attempted.	Media handling could have avoided minor rips or folds. Media or technique was not fully explored. Visual challenges were minimal.	Poor handling or storage had an impact. Media & techniques show little evidence of exploration. Visual challenges were avoided.	____
Original, Personal, & Unique (Always credit your inspirations)	100% original & highly personal because:	Generally personal & unique but inspired by:	Topically personalized & based on:	Topical & highly derivative of:	Copied
Comments:				**Grade**	____

Created by www.artedguru.com & www.FirehousePublications.com

If you could do this project again, what might you do differently?

Project Progress Document   Name _____ pd ____

This paper will document your daily participation, progress, feedback, & grade.

Project Title: _____

My reference or inspirations for this project is: _____

My personal connection: _____

_____

Intro. date   ___/___/_____

DEADLINE: ___/___/_____

Requirements:

1. _____

2. _____

3. _____

To exceed expectations, I can...

1. _____

2. _____

3. _____

Peer Feedback by _____

Actionable advice for success: _____

_____

_____

_____

_____

...Instructor Section Only...	
10% _____	Sketch
20% _____	
25% _____ (quarter)	
30% _____	Project Work Phase
40% _____	
50% _____ (half)	
60% _____	
70% _____	
75% _____ (3/4)	
80% _____	Detail & finishing
85% _____	
90% _____	
95% _____	
(Percent complete, not a grade)	

I will take this advice: [__] Yes or [__] No thank you.

Name _____ Title _____ Pd. _____

Universal Art Project Rubric

	Criteria					Points
	100% / 20pts Exceeds Expectations	90% / 18pts Meets Expectations	80% / 16pts Approaches Exp.	70% - 65% / 14pts Missed Exp.	0/F	
Project Requirements	I exceeded expectations by:	Expected use & combination of art elements & principles. Work included all requirements.	Acceptable use of art elements & principles but lacked depth in exploring requirements.	Lacks evidence of thoughtful use of elements & principles & minimally met required components.		____
Process, Research & Documentation	I exceeded expectations by:	Research & documentation are present & meet expectations. Prewriting & sketches are complete & purposeful.	Research and/or documentation is present but thin. Artist did not fully take advantage of pre-work opportunities.	Research and/or documentation was missing & had a negative impact on the final work. Evidence of depth was lacking.		____
Time & Management	I exceeded expectations by:	Student was mostly independently motivated with a few social and/or digital distractions. Work was mostly self-driven.	Student was sometimes distracted from work **OR** finished early without using the extra time to exceed expectations or stay active in art-making.	Often reminded to stay on task. Social/digital interactions impeded work. Lack of focus had a strong impact on project work.		____
Detail, Complexity, Craftsmanship, & Care	I exceeded expectations by:	Media is without folds/rips or evidence of poor handling. Materials & techniques were explored & met handling expectations. Visual challenges were attempted.	Media handling could have avoided minor rips or folds. Media or technique was not fully explored. Visual challenges were minimal.	Poor handling or storage had an impact. Media & techniques show little evidence of exploration. Visual challenges were avoided.		____
Original, Personal, & Unique (Always credit your inspirations)	100% original & highly personal because:	Generally personal & unique but inspired by:	Topically personalized & based on:	Topical & highly derivative of:	Copied	

Comments:

Grade ____

Created by www.artedguru.com & www.FirehousePublications.com

If you could do this project again, what might you do differently?

Project Progress Document   Name _____ pd ____

This paper will document your daily participation, progress, feedback, & grade.

Project Title: _____

My reference or inspirations for this project is: _____

My personal connection: _____

_____

Intro. date   ___/___/_____

DEADLINE: ___/___/_____

Requirements:

1. _____

2. _____

3. _____

To exceed expectations, I can…

1. _____

2. _____

3. _____

Peer Feedback by _____

Actionable advice for success: _____

_____

...Instructor Section Only...

10% _____   *Sketch*

20% _____

25% _____ (quarter)

30 % _____   *Project Work Phase*

40% _____

50% _____ (half)

60% _____

70% _____

75% _____ (3/4)

80% _____   *Detail & finishing*

85% _____

90% _____

95% _____

(Percent complete, not a grade)

_____

_____

_____

I will take this advice: [__] Yes or [__] No thank you.

Name _____ Title _____ Pd._____

Universal Art Project Rubric

	Criteria				Points
	100% / 20pts Exceeds Expectations	90% / 18pts Meets Expectations	80% / 16pts Approaches Exp.	70% - 65% / 14pts Missed Exp.	0/F
Project Requirements	*I exceeded expectations by:*	Expected use & combination of art elements & principles. Work included all requirements.	Acceptable use of art elements & principles but lacked depth in exploring requirements.	Lacks evidence of thoughtful use of elements & principles & minimally met required components.	____
Process, Research & Documentation	*I exceeded expectations by:*	Research & documentation are present & meet expectations. Prewriting & sketches are complete & purposeful.	Research and/or documentation is present but thin. Artist did not fully take advantage of pre-work opportunities.	Research and/or documentation was missing & had a negative impact on the final work. Evidence of depth was lacking.	____
Time & Management	*I exceeded expectations by:*	Student was mostly independently motivated with a few social and/or digital distractions. Work was mostly self-driven.	Student was sometimes distracted from work **OR** finished early without using the extra time to exceed expectations or stay active in art-making.	Often reminded to stay on task. Social/digital interactions impeded work. Lack of focus had a strong impact on project work.	____
Detail, Complexity, Craftsmanship, & Care	*I exceeded expectations by:*	Media is without folds/rips or evidence of poor handling. Materials & techniques were explored & met handling expectations. Visual challenges were attempted.	Media handling could have avoided minor rips or folds. Media or technique was not fully explored. Visual challenges were minimal.	Poor handling or storage had an impact. Media & techniques show little evidence of exploration. Visual challenges were avoided.	____
Original, Personal, & Unique (Always credit your inspirations)	100% original & highly personal because:	Generally personal & unique but inspired by:	Topically personalized & based on:	Topical & highly derivative of:	Copied

Comments:

Grade ____

Created by www.artedguru.com & www.FirehousePublications.com

If you could do this project again, what might you do differently?

Made in United States
North Haven, CT
13 July 2025